Perspectives in Reading No. 17

SOCIAL PERSPECTIVES ON READING:
Social Influences and Reading Achievement

Compiled and Edited by

James B. Macdonald
University of North Carolina at Greensboro

INTERNATIONAL READING ASSOCIATION
Newark, Delaware 19711

INTERNATIONAL READING ASSOCIATION

OFFICERS
1972-1973

Contents

Contributors

Wayne Berridge
University of Wisconsin at Milwaukee

Rolland Callaway
University of Wisconsin at Milwaukee

James B. Macdonald
University of North Carolina at Greensboro

Alex Molnar
University of Wisconsin at Milwaukee

Will Roy
University of Wisconsin at Milwaukee

Jack Williams
University of Wisconsin at Milwaukee

John Zahorik
University of Wisconsin at Milwaukee

Foreword

Reading is a creature of society. People invented writing when they first felt the need to communicate ideas in a more permanent form than in speech. Thereupon, they simultaneously created the need for interpreting written symbols through a process which came to be called reading.

Over the centuries, writing and its correlate, reading, became highly valued means of communication. Written documents permit society to preserve one manifestation of its cultural heritage. So valued became the written record in the schooling of many societies that education soon became synonymous with learning to read. Thus, those who learned to read became the "educated" elite while others remained "uneducated." This stereotype of education has been rudely jolted, especially by two contemporary developments in society: one, a burgeoning educational technology exemplified by the advent of television, tape-cassettes, and a host of multisensory aids to learning; and two, a crisis in social values which has led to a vigorous emphasis upon direct, rather than vicarious, experience. One consequence of these developments is the need to reappraise, in relation to society's need, the unique and complementary roles of all major ways of learning, including reading.

IRA's charge to the 1972 Perspectives in Reading conference chairman was to examine reading as a social institution in a way designed to elicit audience participation and reaction. Dr. James B. Macdonald enlisted the aid of a team of colleagues to present seven different societal perspectives on reading. Designed to initiate dialogues about reading, the views expressed in this collection of papers are intended to be thought-provoking in nature and far-ranging in scope. I join Dr. Macdonald in the hope that the perspectives offered in this volume may help us to rethink constructively some of our more persistent problems in reading and in the teaching of reading.

Theodore L. Harris, *President*
International Reading Association
1971-1972

Introduction

This monograph might have been subtitled "After the Coleman Report." That is to say, by 1966 and since then, studies and analyses of schooling, and specifically achievement in reading, have clearly shown that social factors which influence schooling are the major single determinants of pupil achievement. Problems now must be redefined in terms of this growing understanding. Methodological salvation is, clearly, no longer a hope or possibility.

The contributors to this monograph are in accord on at least one premise: Teachers of reading are either part of the problem or part of the solution. In most cases we are all part of the problem since we accept this social status quo and the methodological quest for solutions. What this acceptance has done, in effect, is merely to embed us more deeply in the problems we had hoped to solve.

Each contributor attempts to make a point which illuminates a social perspective on reading. Callaway begins the statements with the idea that the teaching of reading must be looked at in terms of educational policy or politics. He raises questions about the basis of many of our decisions that heretofore had been thought to be in terms of scientific data and in the service of the learner.

Williams follows with a semihistorical orientation which traces social class, ethnic, and racial biases on achievement. He suggests that reading achievement is more directly connected to broad social problems than it is to school practices.

Macdonald continues with a broad view of the impact of technology upon culture, and specifically that of television upon reading. He suggests that television will become and probably already is becoming the most important media in our society. Thus, the school's almost total emphasis upon reading as the media for learning is becoming less and less tenable in our society.

Berridge looks specifically at the "reading establishment" as a social phenomenon. He reminds us that the status, roles, rewards, and prestige of our experts in reading can, and in fact do, have a self-perpetuating quality which may interfere with solving our reading problems.

Roy modifies this theme and focuses upon the nature of school bureaucracy and how it may impinge upon reading achievement. He illustrates how the teaching of reading may be modified by bureaucratic and organizational factors.

Zahorik focuses upon social factors in the classroom. He demonstrates how general climate and teacher-pupil interactions impinge upon reading tasks and learning. He raises questions about whether social practices and the kinds of social persons in classrooms may not be antithetical to stated learning goals for reading.

Molnar completes the series with a broader look at the problem of values. He suggests that reading must be seen outside the context of technical problems where the problem of the concomitant teaching of values is put into focus. He emphasizes that the social context of reading demands not only that we go beyond method but that we keep in mind its place in the total development of persons in society.

What will help us? Contributors to this volume make some suggestions, but primarily they provide seven different social views or perspectives which may help us redefine our problems and, hopefully, stimulate us to creative problem solving. Along the way, it is hoped, you will enjoy the ideas and insights presented.

JBM

Social Perspectives on Reading: Politics

Rolland Callaway

The basic premise or concern I wish to discuss is that reading should be examined in the context of policy making and politics: that is, the issues and problems we have regarding reading should be studied and viewed from a political perspective. Educators have ignored the fact that educational decision making is a political activity. This omission is not only absurd, it is destructive.

Politics may be defined as what politicians do, but I would also contend that politics is what people do. We might say consequently, that all people are politicians. I believe that "power" and "conflict" are the inextricable bedfellows of politics. Lasswell (*20*) says, "Power is the opportunity to make decisions and/or choose those who do." So, politics may be thought of as man's use of power to deal with and resolve the conflicts which confront him. I have postulated that reading is in the political arena. Thus a consideration of reading must reflect an awareness of the use of power and the existence of conflict as elements of the political reality involved.

People are taught to read so that they may become more literate. Literacy, however, is a much broader concept than reading. One might say that literacy refers more to living while reading refers more to schooling.

Functional literacy thus includes such notions as good citizenship, being reasonable, and using common sense. Reading, then, appears to be *one* crucial means for achieving an educational level of functional literacy for the population. The skill of reading, consequently, is a critical contribution to the political goal of literacy.

Reading, itself, is difficult to define. One of the most comprehensive discussions of the definition of reading may be found in Gephart's report (*16*) of the USOE Cooperative Research Project: "The Application of the Convergence Technique to Basic Studies of Reading." In Appendix B of this document, Gephart

CALLAWAY

3

describes the difficulties the group had with definition and does an admirable job of discussing various approaches to definition. He notes:

> As the reading planning team worked, it was not uncommon for someone to ask, "What is the definition of reading?" To such a query the reading specialists in the group responded, "The definition depends upon your perspective or interest in reading." . . . Some people are interested in reading as a perceptual task. Their definition is structured around the perceptual process. Others see reading as one way in which meaning can be transmitted from person to person. Their definitions reflect that semantic transfer focus. Those involved in teaching beginning readers may focus on the development of certain visual and auditory language processing skills. Reading is sometimes defined by these people as the generation of such skills.

In the definition approach in the convergence project an interesting distinction was made between *reading* and *reading behaviors.* It seems that both of these should be considered in the definition of reading. After some discussion the participants agreed on the following definition of reading behaviors:

> *Reading behaviors* are covert responses to verbal written language. These
> (1) (2) (4) (5) (3)
> covert responses are indicated by overt performance which could not have
> (7) (6) (8)
> occurred without the covert responses to the written language.

Following a thorough discussion of approaches to a definition, the Gephart report provides the following summary definition of reading:

> "Reading" is a term used to refer to an interaction by which meaning encoded in visual stimuli by an author becomes meaning in the mind of a reader. The interaction always includes three facets: 1) material to be read; 2) knowledge possessed by the reader; and 3) physiological and intellectual activities. The variability apparent when the interaction is viewed at different points in time is a result of the variability possible in each of the several facets.

With the foregoing as background data and from my perspective of this situation, I have identified six postulates which I would like to discuss.

POLITICAL POSTULATES TO PONDER

1. Reading is not so important a life skill as it used to be. (Maybe it never was.)

I am sure I do not need to plague you with quotations from McLuhan (*22*) and Gattegno (*15*) explaining that this is a multimedia world. Some people wonder how we can continue to ignore this fact. I think we must also note that there are political ramifications in this ignorance. Why do we persist in it?

Social Perspectives on Reading: Politics

As I have intimated in the definitions, my discussion of the importance of reading is heavily flavored with a difference between reading and literacy. My basic concern is with the practical, utilitarian question: How much reading does the average man or woman need to do in order to live a rather comfortable participatory life? Is reading an eternal verity in the good life? Is it a critical element and skill? Is the publisher's advertising slogan "Reading Makes Life Easier" really true?

In this question of the importance of reading I would like to include the emphasis placed on reading in the process of schooling, We might go back as far as to the scholastics, the first to employ a method of structuring and presenting material. The basis of scholastic instruction was the lecture—but along came the printing press and the book. A dilemma! Once the lecturer put all of the questions and answers in a book the dialectic, the logical thinking, and the discussion were left out and the students simply studied and learned the answers. While this process tended to bring about the disputation (debate following lectures) and lectures with summarization and comments on texts, reading the text came to be the universe of the student. And as for the lecturer, Broudy points out:

> The textmakers seem to be in constant pursuit of the lecturer—intent on making him superfluous and often succeeding without the victim's being aware of it (*14*).

I believe we must seriously examine the process of schooling in regard to the basic goals and objectives of the school. And I particularly want to question the emphasis on reading as related to the more general goals and objectives that many of us like to talk about and hold to. Perhaps my point can be illustrated with a personal experience of several years ago. I was working with a group of teachers on the utilization of television in the classroom. One of Shakespeare's plays was scheduled on a local television channel, and I suggested to an English teacher that she have her students view the play and discuss it in class. She agreed that viewing it would probably be all right but certainly the viewing would not substitute for reading the play. Should failure in reading mean failure in schooling?

In this question of the importance of reading I refer to two sources which may help in analyzing the situation. First, consider Smith, Stanley, and Shores (*27*) who in their classic text on *Fundamentals of Curriculum Development* have a chapter on "The Validation of Educational Objectives." It seems to me we might apply their criteria of "Social Adequacy," "Basic Human Needs," "Democratic Ideals," "Consistency and Noncontradiction," and "Behavioristic Interpretation" to the reading goal. By the way, the application of such criteria is a political activity. A second source is Kirst and Walker's "An Analysis of Curriculum Policy-Making" (*19*). They state:

> Among the most important of the specifically educational policies of the schools are those pertaining to what children study in school. Children in school are normally required to study certain subjects and forbidden to study others, encouraged to pursue some topics and discouraged from

pursuing others, provided with opportunities to study some phenomena but not provided with the means to study others. When these requirements and pressures are uniformly and consistently operative they amount to policy, whether we intended so or not. We shall call such explicit or implicit "guides to action" *curriculum policy* and the process of arriving at such policy we shall call *curriculum policy-making*.

When first reading this matter I had the urge to say, "Yeah, but policy making is political activity!" But, in a backhanded way, the authors Kirst and Walker said it for me:

Yet when professional educators write about or study the curriculum, they rarely conceive of their subject in political terms.

My first postulate, then, raises the question of the importance of reading in a multimedia culture—and the relative importance of reading as a goal and medium of schooling in a multimedia culture. Shades of motherhood and apple pie!

2. *The emphasis which is placed on reading as a life skill is a function of cultural elitism rather than utility.*

My second postulate is closely allied to the first. It is my contention that the political pressures which permeate the reading emphasis can be attributed to cultural elitism. To put it simply, the "good guys" can read; the "bad guys" cannot. Or, in elitist terms, the good guys should and the bad guys shouldn't. In a sense, reading has become the *sign* of the middle and upper classes. Reading has been identified as a critical element in social mobility. (But as stated earlier, this identification may well be a red herring.) It does not seem to matter whether reading is necessary; it is simply *required* to get up the ladder—to go to college or to get a good job. This situation might be described as "the reading ethic"—a sort of cultural elitism which means you are a second class citizen if you cannot read.

I think the reading ethic can be compared to the familiar work ethic; that is, work is good—leisure is not good. I think I can best illustrate my point by reference to an insightful article by Nolen (*23*) who, at the time of this writing, was a high school senior. Titled "Coming of Age in a Work-Oriented World," the article points out how difficult it is to "come to grips" with maturity in a culture where some of the attitudes have their basis in preindustrial revolution times although "the times" have shifted from an agrarian to an industrial society. Nolen notes that this new society has created demands for intellect and training—for an increasing length of time which the young spend in schools.

Eventually, the idea of child labor was replaced with public schooling and education for youths. A compulsory school attendance age was established. Education enabled individuals to obtain more favorable positions in the working world, even if it meant entering the job market a little later than other persons. . . . The problem is that, unless one enters the working world and is accepted under the working world ethic, one hardly knows when one is "grown up." It is bothersome, to say the least, to be unsure as to whether society accepts you as an adult.

Yet, with the importance of education increasing, "How is society to deal with youths who prefer to brush past the 'make it or break it' economic world and find maturity in education? . . . With education constantly increasing in importance, a greater number of persons will bypass the traditional ritual of coming of age in their first employment experience and will mature in a learning situation" (23). What a nasty question and thought—and a political one at that.

But I would return to my contention that the reading ethic may be related to the work ethic in respect to Nolen's concern for some definition of maturity. If maturity is to be arrived at in education, I do hope education is *more* than reading. I hope education and schooling are made up of more than the reading ethic—more than book-larnin'. Let me try to be more explicit about the political implications in terms of a person's coming of age. As a young person I should want to work—for it is good to work. But I cannot work, so I go to school—for it is good to become intelligent and trained, which essentially means "socialized" so that when I do become a worker, I will know how to behave. I should learn to be punctual, to do a good day's work for a good day's pay, to write legibly, and to *read* well. (At least at the sixth grade level as one telephone company executive recently implored. I wonder if he has the slightest notion what that means— reading the company newsletter? or *Time*? or the *New York Times*? or what?) So when youngsters go to school (either because they want to go or are compelled to), they must read, for that is what school is all about. It is about books and reading and remembering what has been read (at least until the test). Every youngster quickly recognizes that real education is what you have left after you have forgotten all you have learned.

Finally, in respect to reading and cultural elitism, I refer to a comment of Loving (21):

America is divided by its many subcultures. Each of these groups does make a contribution to the total of the American culture. But emphasis on any one of them or any few of them could delay the development of a *basic* American culture. Schools must recognize that much of their difficulty, whether it is at the local level or at the state level, has been promulgated by many of the subgroups of our American culture. Again to quote J. A. Battle, "Without a politics of education that is intelligently led and altruistically based, there can be little hope for gaining quality education in a democracy."

I, for one, hope that reading and the reading cult are not seen as the only means for developing a basic American culture. I also hope that we do not continue to use reading as a means of keeping our subcultures divided.

3. Because of what is known about child growth and development, reading should not be taught until the chronological age of ten to eleven.

I will assume that the readers of this paper have knowledge of child growth and development; that is, they have studied Gesell, Piaget, etc. Thus, I will not attempt to be specific in my discussion of this postulate. (I am sure some will accuse me of being too general and too simplistic.) My basic point is that the emphasis prompted by the importance of reading (postulate 1) and reading as a must for the cultured person (postulate 2) has been the critical consideration in determining reading programs. The political decisions that people have made in regard to postulates 1 and 2 have led us to ignore to a large extent what we know about how children grow and develop. (These political actions in determining programs should also be related to postulate 4, the methodological debate; postulate 5, the word attack versus thinking situation; and postulate 6, the reading establishment and industry thing.) Please let it be known that I do not place the blame on any one group. We are all to blame—we have all had our political reading axes to grind. So, suffer the little children.

In this context is an article by Welsh (*29*) concerning research projects:

> ... any institution receiving HEW money for research projects must estab-
> lish review boards that will assume the responsibility for making sure that
> "subjects" of the research are protected from physical-psychological risk,
> invasion of privacy, and breakdown of confidentiality. ... In the educa-
> tion area we find that in most places, parents expect the schools to control
> what investigations are conducted. Ours is a thrust to get the institutions
> sponsoring the research to be more responsible, to schools, to the parents
> and to the children.

Great! When we look at the vast number of reading projects that have been foisted upon youngsters, I say it is time someone looked at the goals and strate-gies in relation to what we know about child growth and development—and to children's dignity as well. Maybe kids need a reading ombudsman.

I also believe that we need to pay much more attention to reading in relation to the total language development of children. I believe that reading has been overemphasized—because of the political pressures—to the extent that a full language arts, communications curriculum is practically impossible to mount. I like very much one of the concluding comments of Chomsky (*9*) in her report on a study of "Stages in Language Development and Reading Exposure."

> Our reading results indicate that exposure to the more complex language
> available from reading does not seem to go hand in hand with increased
> knowledge of the language. This would imply that perhaps wider reading
> should find a place in the curriculum. The child could be read to, stimu-
> lated to read on his own, not restricted to material deemed "at his level"
> but permitted access to books well "above his level" to get out of them
> whatever he may. Perhaps he should be encouraged to skim when he reads,
> to skip uninteresting portions and get to the "good parts" instead of
> concentrating at length on controlled texts. In general, it may be that the
> effort should be towards providing more and richer language exposure,

rather than limiting the child with restricting and carefully programmed materials. In this way the child would be permitted to derive what is accessible to him from a wide range of inputs, and put it to use in his own way. This approach would seem to be more closely in accord with the nature of language acquisition as we are coming to understand it.

Now I know there are those who will say that the foregoing is what a good teacher does anyway. It is my contention that all teachers and administrators have been politically pressured to do it the other way.

Another point worth mentioning about reading and child growth and development concerns the multimedia approach—the utilization of a wide variety of media and materials. First, I refer to an article by Barnes (3) whose ideas are extremely helpful in looking at the reading situation. He presents a model for material selection and use which *does* take into account child growth and development and what is known about learning. Barnes poses four assumptions:

> . . . in situations where the pupil is naive, learning proceeds best from concrete, direct experiences and materials.

> . . . in situations where the pupil is mature, learning proceeds most efficiently from symbolic materials.

> . . . continuity in school learning may be found in the pupil's directional growth from naivete to maturity.

> . . . the continuity factor is of prime importance both in relatively short-range, specific learning situations and also in general, long-range maturing toward adult levels of performance.

New? Startling? Of course not! But one wonders why one can't seem to apply these assumptions if they are valid, and I believe they are.

The suggestion that a multimedia approach be utilized raises the problem of obtaining adequate materials. Let's face it. Our experience tells us that where there is money to be spent either for books or for media, the books win out—as enterprising salesmen for new media companies find out to their dismay. And remember these are political decisions. Summerfield (28) makes an important observation in this regard:

> Thus, the inequality of material resource allocations among schools apparently tells more about the politics of education than about the education of children.

Let's begin to base the political decisions that we make about reading on what we know about child growth and development.

4. The methodological debate should be put to bed—buried once and for all.

My basic point concerning the methodological debate is that we have been so obsessed with the methods and means that we have forgotten the ends. The frantic methods game has provided a symptom game for the establishment and the bureaucracy to play so that they don't get involved with the basic problem. From what I have been able to figure out, there just "ain't no" best method of teaching reading. (What I keep alluding to is an approach which would allow children *to learn* to read.)

A report of a recent Educational Testing Service study (*17*) of 1,800 documents on reading, released between 1960 and 1970, states: "It may be possible for students to improve their achievements in reading, but it is unlikely that educators can find a better way to teach it." I am reminded of the wag who wrote in the letters-to-the-editor column of *The Tulsa Tribune,* "There's one happy thought about the schools' teaching sex. If they teach sex as efficiently as they teach reading, the population explosion will be solved, for this generation won't even know how." Now there's a political statement. That person knows—and will vote accordingly—his perceptions of what the schools are for. The ETS study discovered that not only has no better way to teach reading been found but also that most teachers practice an eclectic approach—the best of all possible worlds. This point is well illustrated in the *New York Times* report (*2*) of a program developed by Cureton and evidently tried with success in the Newark schools:

> The system uses the phonic method as the basic means of instruction but relies heavily on "insistence by teachers that the children learn."
>
> It is very action oriented, an official with the Metropolitan Applied Research Center said today. "There is emphasis on the child as an individual and, in the group, with faster children helping slower children."

The ETS study is also critical of teacher training institutions. Why not? Politically, they are a perfect scapegoat. As Harold Hand has said, "A good scapegoat must be where you can hit it, have no money, and have some things wrong with it." My point, then, in belaboring this methodology question is that not only is it a matter for teacher educators and administrators and teachers, it also has been and will continue to be a political football. I know. I was a school principal when Sputnik went up. Remember when Johnny couldn't read? Or was there ever a time when he could?

5. The reading problem is essentially a comprehension-thinking-interest problem rather than the mechanistic, word attack and word analysis problem the reading establishment would have us believe.

Instruction in and development of reading as a basic skill have dominated the elementary school curriculum. As was indicated in postulate 5, the time and the effort of many people have been focused on discovering the *best* method to teach reading (not necessarily the best way for children to learn it). The political pressures in regard to the problems have resulted in all kinds of special remedial programs and projects. In my humble opinion, most of them are designed to deal with the symptom rather than the problem. We tend to use the More Principle in utilizing methods—if a little is good, more is bound to be better.

I would suggest that, other than in some very basic and critical cases (and I do not minimize those), most of the reading problem that we talk about is in reality that of comprehension-thinking-interest. Very simply put, a child may perceptually be able to decode a message, but he may have no background—no experiences—which help him do anything with the ability. Or to present the more complex problem, he may just not be interested in doing anything with it. I think "listening" as a communication skill provides an analogy. (But interestingly enough we don't get "up tight" about listening.) We have made great strides in studying the problems of cognition, concept development, etc. But it seems to me when we get to teaching reading, we become so anxious and defensive (perhaps because of political pressures) that we ignore what we know about children and learning. There was a good, old cliche in the days of Progressive Education (whatever that was) which said "the whole child goes to school." We might do well to contemplate that cliche. The whole child does go to school—not just the reading child.

6. *The reading establishment and industry, as contenders in the political arena, are caught up in a self-fulfilling prophesy.*

Although Berridge deals with the establishment as the specific topic of his paper, this writer's position here demands at least a brief comment about the reading establishment and the reading industry.

I have attempted to establish the fact that there are critical political aspects in the decisions which are made in regard to reading and the educational enterprise in general. My concern is that we recognize the extent to which those who are of the reading establishment and reading industry are involved in the decisions made about reading and reading programs. (Remember politics includes the elements of power and conflict.) In this postulate, I wish to emphasize my concern about a self-fulfilling prophecy. Perhaps this concern is more succinctly expressed by Wirsing (*30*):

> A narcissistic attitude promotes the almost unconscious desire to *facilitate change* in *one's own direction*. The individual [or group, or industry] so afflicted wants all others to reflect what he himself holds to be good and desirable. Having others around him thinking and doing whatever he is thinking and doing undoubtedly supports him in his conviction that he is *right*. [Parentheses and insertion mine.]

My concern, which is personified by the Right to Read cult and the publishing industry, can be illustrated best by slogans such as:

"Reading makes life easier."
"You've got a right to read. Don't blow it."
"Learning to read is every child's right."

I guess I would be a little more comfortable if these slogans were broader in concept—perhaps referring to education rather than reading. But before someone else reminds me, I realize this is a narcissistic attitude on my part.

Another concern I have in connection with the establishment and industry has to do with what children are required to read or permitted to read. This is, of course, a political situation. First, there is the familiar whole textbook-selection process which is about as political as one can get. Then there is the whole question of what ideas, topics, and issues are to appear in the books which young people read and study. Here I refer you to the delightful, but frightening, *The American Schoolbook* (5). We must continue to recognize and struggle with the political implications of the selection and the content question.

CONCLUSIONS AND RECOMMENDATIONS

I conclude with what might be titled "An Immodest Proposal" or "A Narcissistic Proposal." I am reminded of what Popham (24) said at a symposium on behavioral objectives:

> I would prefer unanimous support of the position to which I subscribe. You see the other people are wrong. Adhering to a philosophic tenet that error is evil, I hate to see my friends wallowing in sin.

I fully recognize that this proposal will not be an overnight accomplishment. But I believe we must begin—and with the following basic propositions and commitments:

1. Work toward decreasing the emphasis on formal teaching of reading until the chronological age of ten or eleven.
2. Insist that schooling consist of a multimedia approach—at all levels, but particularly at the early childhood and early adolescent levels.
3. Stress approaches which emphasize reading in relation to comprehension, thinking, and interest rather than the rote learning of words and word attack skills.
4. Pay more attention to the political aspects of decision making in regard to reading and reading programs. [I want to give special credit to Postman (25) in regard to this point—and in the development of this paper.]

In summary, I believe that the development of reading and reading programs is a political ball game—no, "battle" is a better word. For the sake of kids and humaneness I believe those of us in education should pay more attention to this battle. We should realize it involves the elements of power and conflict. I have said a bit about who the contenders are—the establishment, the industry, the bureaucracy, the teachers, the parents. I have intimated that children are not contenders but unsuspecting victims. If there is a Right to Read, is there a Right Not to Read? "Right" is a political term. More specifically, I have said 1) that reading is overrated as to importance as a life skill, 2) that reading and literacy should not be considered as synonymous, 3) that we attempt to teach reading too early in a child's life, 4) that there has been too much concentration on methodology instead of what reading is, and 5) that reading has been wrongly treated as a scapegoat for all of the ills of the school and the society. Finally, I have referred to the emphasis on reading as a function of cultural elitism. Perhaps this should be viewed as my most serious point, for it has to do with our cultural and social crises. If reading represents a case of cultural and societal schizophrenia, we should get it out in the open and examine it.

References and Notes

1. Allen, Gary G. "Right to Read: Rhetoric or Reality," *Phi Delta Kappan,* 52 (December 1971), 217-220.
2. Andelman, David A. "New Plan Raises Reading Levels," *New York Times,* March 8, 1972, 1.
3. Barnes, Fred P. "Materials of Learning—and Learning," *Educational Leadership,* 9 (April 1952), 402-408.
4. Battle, J. A. *Culture and Education for the Contemporary World.* Columbus, Ohio: Charles E. Merrill, 1969.
5. Black, Hillel. *The American Schoolbook.* New York: Morrow, 1967.
6. Bodcock, Sarane S. *An Introduction to the Sociology of Learning.* Boston: Houghton Mifflin, 1972.
7. Boulding, Kenneth E. "The Schooling Industry as a Possible Pathological Section of the American Economy," *Review of Educational Research,* 42 (Winter 1972), 129-143.
8. "Breaking the American Stereotypes," *Time,* February 1972, 36-41.
9. Chomsky, Carol. "Stages in Language Development and Reading Exposure," *Harvard Educational Review,* 42 (February 1972), 1-33.
10. "Coleman on the Coleman Report," *Educational Researcher,* 1 (March 1972), 13-14.
11. Dentler, Robert A., and Mary Ellen Warshauer. *Big City Dropouts and Illiterates.* New York: Frederick A. Prager, 1968.
12. Duggins, James. "The Right to Read: Target for the 70s," *Phi Delta Kappan,* 52 (April 1971), 457-459.
13. Engler, David. "Instructional Technology and the Curriculum," *Phi Delta Kappan,* 51 (March 1970), 379-381.
14. Gage, Nathaniel Lees. *Handbook of Research on Teaching.* Chicago: Rand McNally, 1963.
15. Gattegno, Caleb. *Towards a Visual Culture.* New York: Avon Books, 1969.
16. Gephart, William J. *Application of the Convergence Technique to Basic Studies of the Reading Process.* Washington, D. C.: U. S. Department of Health, Education and Welfare, Office of Education, National Center for Educational Research and Development, 1970 (Project Number 8-0737).
17. "Is There a Better Way to Teaching?" *TEAM.* Milwaukee, Wisconsin: Milwaukee Teachers' Education Association (*Education U.S.A.* reprint).
18. Jacobs, Leland B. "Humanism in Teaching Reading," *Phi Delta Kappan,* 52 (April 1971), 464-467.
19. Kirst, Michael W., and Decker F. Walker. "An Analysis of Curriculum Policy-Making," *Review of Educational Research,* 41 (December 1971), 479-509.
20. Lasswell, Harold. From the film "Social Process and Institutions."

21. Loving, Alvin D. "Political Power, the School, and the Culture," *Educational Leadership,* 28 (October 1970), 7-8.
22. McLuhan, Marshall. *The Gutenberg Galaxy.* New York: New American Library, 1969.
23. Nolen, Pamela. "Coming of Age in a Work-Oriented World," *Educational Leadership,* 29 (December 1971), 234-236.
24. Popham, W. James. "Probing the Validity of Arguments Against Behavioral Objectives," presentation at the Annual American Education Research Association Meeting, Chicago, 1968.
25. Postman, Neil. "The Politics of Reading," *Harvard Educational Review,* 40 (May 1970), 244-252.
26. "Right to Read: New Director, New Approach," *Phi Delta Kappan,* 53 (December 1971), 221-224.
27. Smith, B. Othanel, William O. Stanley, and J. Harlan Shores. *Fundamentals of Curriculum Development.* Yonkers-on-Hudson, New York: World, 1957.
28. Summerfield, Harry L. *The Neighborhood-based Politics of Education.* Columbus, Ohio: Charles E. Merrill, 1971.
29. Welsh, James. "Protecting Research Subjects: A New HEW Policy," *Educational Researcher,* 1 (March 1972), 11-12.
30. Wirsing, Marie E. "Narcissism and the Process of Education," *Houghton Mifflin Education News,* 17.

Racism: The Fourth R

Jack E. Williams

A theory of instruction is a political theory in the proper sense that it derives from consensus concerning the distribution of power within the society—who shall be educated and to fulfill what roles? In the very same sense, pedagogical theory must surely derive from a conception of economics, for where there is division of labor within the society and an exchange of goods and services for wealth and prestige, then *how* people are educated and in what numbers and with what constraints on the use of resources are all relevant issues. The psychologist or educator who formulates pedagogical theory without regard to the political, economic, and social setting of the educational process courts triviality and merits being ignored in the community and in the classroom.

—Jerome S. Bruner
Saturday Review, May 18, 1968

In his preface to *The Doctor's Dilemma,* Shaw (9) wryly observes, "Thus it is easy to prove that the wearing of tall hats and the carrying of umbrellas enlarges the chest, prolongs life, and confers comparative immunity from disease; for the statistics show that the classes which use these articles are bigger, healthier, and live longer than the class which never dreams of possessing such things." Shaw's insightful perception concerning the nature of cause and effect relationships typifies the thinking and research of numerous American citizens who believe that academic achievement, as it has been traditionally defined, is the fundamental prerequisite to socioeconomic success.

For decades, studies have indicated an astounding correlation between socioeconomic status and academic achievement. In 1947, for example, the President's Commission on Higher Education noted, "For the great majority of our boys and girls, the kind and amount of education they may hope to attain depends, not on their own abilities, but on the family or community into which they happened to be born or, worse still, on the color of their skin or the religion of their parents" (7). More recent studies—the 1966 Coleman Report, for example—continue to reiterate these conclusions. Thus, to maintain the belief that low academic achievement is the cause rather than the consequence of poverty and unemployment will only further enhance the ambiguity and the anxiety that prevent significant social change.

SCHOOLING, SOCIAL MOBILITY, AND THE LABOR MARKET

The growing concern about academic achievement obscures the fact that more than 90 percent of the students in 1915 failed to complete high school. Although these individuals may have been considered "culturally deprived or disadvantaged," their academic failure generally was not viewed to be a crisis issue in education. They dropped out, either by choice or necessity, and joined the labor force. Since the turn of the century, however, the structure of the labor market has been altered significantly. The twentieth century has witnessed the continuing decline of the traditional vocational opportunities in agriculture and industry and the rapid emergence of bureaucratization, automation, and professionalization.

Public schooling historically has been closely interrelated with the labor market. When job opportunities were readily available, schooling, for the majority of American citizens, was the alternative to the work force; and when jobs are scarce, the work force is the alternative to schooling. With fewer job opportunities individuals encounter the prospect of unemployment or extended periods of formal schooling; and, as occupational options to schooling continue to decline, the importance of schooling is enhanced. Credentials attained through formal education have become the prerequisite not only for employment but also for job promotion. The social consequences of this trend are described by the sociologist Caplow: ". . . within the last half-century, formal education has become the principal channel of upward mobility in the Western world. The distribution of educational opportunities thus becomes a crucial factor in determining how much movement between social classes will be permitted" (1). In contrast to previous generations, an individual who fails in school fails in life.

The relationship of academic achievement to social mobility is of critical concern to members of racial and/or ethnic minorities and especially to those of the lower socioeconomic strata. Historically these groups have encountered persistent failure in the classroom. Speaking before the Massachusetts Convention of Teachers in 1876, Andrew Peabody expressed a sentiment concerning racial and/or ethnic minorities that continues to be shared by many individuals involved in public schooling. Discussing the problem of educating the children of immigrants, he asserted, "A very large proportion of the pupils in our cities and populous towns come from homes utterly destitute of culture and of the means and the spirit of culture, where a book is never seen and reading is with the adult members a lost art or one never acquired" (6). Nearly a century later Peabody's view of the Irish in Boston is reflected in the educational literature. The groups being characterized, however, are no longer Irish or Italian. It is presently the Black, the Puerto Rican, the Indian, the Mexican, or the Appalachian that is labeled "culturally deprived" or "culturally disadvantaged." In fact, these terms are utilized to describe nearly any poor, lower-class individual or group, regardless of racial and/or ethnic origin. Lower-class individuals now are termed "deprived" rather than "depraved"; the fear of mixing mental capacities has replaced the fear of mixing blood lines; and environmental bias and institutional racism have supplanted personal prejudice.

Numerous attempts have been made to differentiate between the middle-class values of teachers and the lower-class values of minority group students. Many textbooks, reflecting, perhaps, the class bias of the authors, depict middle-class values in terms of the protestant ethic—thrift, self-reliance, initiative, honesty, perseverance, and hard work. Opposing values are attributed to members of the lower class. Such an analysis, however, fails to consider the changing value orientation in modern middle-class America. In an age of automation and credit cards, leisure and consumption have generally replaced hard work and thrift. Also, such an analysis fails to acknowledge the fact that many individuals of lower socioeconomic status diligently practice the virtues attributed to the middle class. Migrant farm workers, for example, certainly work harder than the overwhelming majority of the middle class; and welfare recipients, to survive on such a minimal income, must demonstrate thrift and perseverance. To acknowledge the fact that members of the lower class share many of the values and aspirations of the middle class is to take the first step in solving many of our socioeconomic and educational problems.

A more fruitful analysis, perhaps, would focus upon middle-class attitudes, rather than middle-class values. For example, the condescending, if not contemptuous, attitude toward lower-class individuals, illustrated in the statement by Peabody, serves to create conflict and diminish any possibility of establishing mutual respect. Individuals who are perceived as "uneducable heathens" invariably become so. This pseudoaristocratic attitude, at best patronizing, is demonstrated by many middle-class teachers when they encounter differences in language patterns, personal dress and hair śtyles, and perceptions of authority. For too many teachers, the concern for "manners" inhibits effective teaching and learning. This type of authoritarianism not only refuses to acknowledge the benefits of cultural pluralism but it also denies the basic human values of tolerance, empathy, and understanding.

Although academic achievement provided a bootstrap for a few of their members, the vast majority of the lower-class individuals were forced to seek economic stability and social mobility in small business ventures, unions, and political machines. As Greer (4) so aptly observes, "Economic stability for an ethnic group preceded its entry onto the broader middle-class stage via education." Middle-class socioeconomic status generally precedes academic success rather than follows from it. Just as graduation from certain private schools has symbolized the attainment of upper-middle-class socioeconomic status, graduation from public schools has symbolized the attainment of middle and lower middle-class socioeconomic status. Seldom have either private or public schools functioned as bootstraps to lift one from the bottom of the social structure.

The relationship of formal education to social mobility creates additional obstacles to the aspirations of many lower-class members. Obviously the cost of formal schooling has been prohibitive to the poor. The close correlation between an individual's economic status and the level of schooling he attains has been carefully documented by numerous scholars, most notably, perhaps, by Sexton (8). The economic value of an education, however, has been not only the cause but also the consequence of its scarcity. There is no guarantee, therefore, that the credential an individual receives by demonstrating a certain level of academic achievement has any inherent worth. The ranks of the unemployed are rapidly being filled with individuals having high school diplomas. Even college graduates have become quite concerned about the availability of job opportunities. In fact, as the number of college graduates continues to grow, the value of the diploma will be increasingly dependent upon the prestige of the university the individual attended. Thus, although two-year colleges provide an educational opportunity for an increasing number of students, such institutions also serve to perpetuate and perhaps promote a socioeconomic class structure. Consequently, even if lower-class students do attain a higher level of academic achievement, their position in society will not necessarily be altered significantly. Equal opportunity is of minimal significance for those individuals who begin the socioeconomic race years, if not generations, after others have started.

NEOPROGRESSIVISM AND VOCATIONALISM

Many, perhaps the majority, of the previous observations noted in this paper have been founded upon historical trends or precedents. The continuing credential orientation of a technological society and the fact that schools persistently have failed the vast majority of lower-class students are representative examples. To reject these apparent historical inevitabilities and to reassert the belief that mankind has the ability to control his destiny require a persistent faith in the nature of man. To accomplish this arduous but essential task, those involved in the educational process must transcend the limitations imposed by the prevalent ideological views that influence American education. Both ideologies, neoprogressivism and vocationalism, fail to provide the elements necessary for social change.

There is a tendency today, especially among upper middle-class neoprogressive educators, to dismiss the importance of academic achievement, in general, and the ability to read and write, in particular. For these individuals, whose prestige in society has been rather firmly established, such accomplishments are often simply assumed. Such persons live in comfortable environments (or self-chosen poverty) and generally espouse an educational philosophy that implies "doing one's own thing." As a result of their middle-class status, members of their families are not threatened with the humiliation and degradation that accompany failure in school and in society. Consequently, it is foolish, if not hypocritical, for an individual with several academic degrees to deny their significance in a credential-oriented society. If an individual truly believes that grades and academic credits are not important, he should exert effort to impose this view on employers and college admissions officials. Until the individuals with power accept such a proposition, however, members of the lower class rightfully can be expected to remain quite concerned about attaining credentials.

In contrast to the neoprogressivists, the vocationalists have focused upon skills and the conventionally accepted definition of academic achievement in their belief that these are prerequisites for meeting the prevailing demands of the socioeconomic system. Any form of schooling, however, whose major focus rests upon the achievement of skills in reading and writing with only a minimal concern for creativity, critical thought, personal identity, and social awareness is merely a training exercise for the preparation of bureaucratic functionaries and technocrats. Obviously these occupations are necessary for the maintenance of a technological society; and, as noted previously, individuals threatened by the prospects of unemployment and welfare can be expected to concur with the more ardent proponents of bureaucratic training. Such a narrow-minded view of education, however, reflects the inadequacies inherent in the educational philosophy of vocationalism espoused by Booker T. Washington, a philosophy that emphasizes the necessity of personal adjustment to the demands of society.

The limitations of the traditional philosophy of vocationalism become more apparent as business and industry are increasingly automated. In a rapidly changing labor structure, it is difficult, if not impossible, to predetermine the vocation skills necessary for employment. In addition, for the vast majority of vocations the prerequisite credential is of much greater significance than the prerequisite skill. In modern technological societies, individuals are vastly overtrained. Credentials often function merely as criteria for employment and job placement, and seldom reflect prerequisite competencies. And finally, those who advocate the need for vocationalism should ask themselves if they would be satisfied with such training. Would they advocate this form of education for their own children? Is *training* an adequate substitute for *education*?

EDUCATION AND SOCIAL CHANGE

Certainly not everyone who expresses a concern for the attainment of basic skills wishes to prepare students for lower positions in the vocational hierarchy. Many individuals obviously realize that higher scores on national achievement tests enhance the possibility of college admissions. Increased academic achievement, however, is only a partial explanation for the growing number of racial and/or ethnic minority members on the college campus. (The significance of Head Start and other compensatory programs has been, no doubt, minimal.) The increasing number of minority students is the result, in part, of their militancy, their emphasis upon identity and political awareness, and their affirmation of the traditional American belief in man's ability to determine his destiny. College officials, consequently, have been forced to reexamine their policies of admissions, hiring, and recruiting.

The importance of an education that enhances a student's personal identity and social awareness has been acknowledged by numerous educators. DuBois, for example, in contrast to those individuals who espouse an ideology of vocationalism, advocates a classical, liberal, education for black youth. He accepts the argument of realists who believe that individuals should acquire the skills necessary for economic survival. "Nevertheless," DuBois (*3*) profoundly observes, "I insist that the object of all true education is not to make men carpenters, it is to make carpenters men . . . ." DuBois' insight obviously could be applied to the education of future computer programers, laboratory technicians, dentists, professors, and reading teachers.

Although Washington's and DuBois' philosophies disagree about the aims of education, they do agree that the acquisition of skills should be a means to an end. With the increasing emphasis upon national testing, in a society enamored with statistics and competition, there is a tendency to perceive reading achievement as an end in itself, rather than as a means to an end. This tendency is enhanced by anti-intellectual attitudes inherent in American thought. As a result, educators tend to focus upon developing the *ability* to read, rather than the *love* of reading—a love that emanates from the understanding of human existence. The universities, consequently, continue to certify reading teachers, many of whom seldom read—a behavioral pattern that appears to be transferred to many American citizens.

CONCLUSION

Since its inception the educational system has mirrored the structure and the ideological commitment of the American society. The question, *Dare the Schools Build a New Social Order?*, raised by the educator George S. Counts in 1932, generally has been answered with a resounding "No!"—an answer vociferously reiterated recently by opponents of busing. In fact, the schools often have been a reactionary force in the society. Periodic calls for relevance have emanated not from revolutionaries but from reformists who desire a readjustment of the school system to more accurately reflect changing social norms. As mirrors of society, consequently, the schools reflect the racial, ethnic, and/or class prejudices inherent in the social structure.

The increasing importance of formal education has enhanced the power of the schools. Institutional changes within the educational system and, more importantly, attitudinal changes within individuals involved in the educational process could aid in the creation of a new social order. Without profound changes in the institutions that control the social, economic, and political forces in this country, however, the realization of this ideal will be impossible; and those involved in the educational process will continue to be used as scapegoats for the ills inherent in American society. Without a firm commitment to guarantee such fundamental rights as employment, housing, medical care, and an adequate income, the problem of academic achievement will continue to exemplify an issue of misplaced relevance.

The educational system, without question, has been an important institution in American society; it has not, however, been a panacea for social ills. It may, at best, serve as a doctor, but it lacks the healing powers of an omnipotent being.

More than four generations have passed since Horace Mann, expressing the American faith in public schooling, proclaimed education to be "... beyond all other devices of human origin, the great equalizer of the conditions of men ..." (5). Yet, in 1967, Clark sadly observed, "... American public education is organized and functions along social and economic class lines .... American public schools have become significant instruments in the blocking of economic mobility and in their intensification of class distinctions rather than fulfilling their historic function of facilitating such mobility" (2). The reality described by Clark must be altered to reflect the ideal expressed by Mann if the hopes and dreams of many American citizens are to be actualized.

Suggested Reading List

Bendix, Reinhard, and Seymour Martin Lipset. *Class, Status and Power—A Reader in Social Stratification.* Glencoe, Illinois: Free Press, 1953.

Clark, Burton R. *Educating the Expert Society.* San Francisco: Chandler Publishing, 1962.

Glazer, Nathan, and Daniel Patrick Moynihan. *Beyond the Melting Pot.* Cambridge, Massachusetts: M.I.T. Press, 1963.

Gordon, Milton M. *Assimilation in American Life.* New York: Oxford University Press, 1964.

Gottlieb, David, and Anne Lienhard Heinsohn. *America's Other Youth—Growing Up Poor.* Englewood Cliffs, New Jersey: Prentice-Hall, 1971.

Harrington, Michael. *The Other America—Poverty in the United States.* Baltimore, Maryland: Penguin Books, 1962.

Herriott, Robert E., and Nancy Hoyt St. John. *Social Class and the Urban School.* New York: John Wiley & Sons, 1966.

Lane, W. Clayton. *Permanence and Change in Social Class: Readings in Stratification.* Cambridge, Massachusetts: Schenkman Publishing, 1968.

Perkinson, Henry J. *The Imperfect Panacea: American Faith in Education, 1865-1965.* New York: Random House, 1968.

Weber, Max. "The Chinese Literati," in H. H. Gerth and C. Wright Mills (Eds.), *From Max Weber: Essays in Sociology.* New York: Oxford University Press, 1958.

References

1. Caplow, Theodore. *The Sociology of Work.* New York: McGraw-Hill, 1954, 27.
2. Clark, Kenneth. "Alternative Public School Systems: A Response to America's Educational Emergency," paper prepared for National Conference on Equal Educational Opportunity in America's Cities, sponsored by U. S. Commission on Civil Rights, Washington, D. C., 1967, 199-200.
3. DuBois, W.E.B. "The Talented Tenth," *The Negro Problem.* New York: James Pott Company, 1903, 63.
4. Greer, Colin. "Immigrants, Negroes, and the Public Schools," *Urban Review,* 3 (January 1969), 9-12.
5. Mann, Horace. *Life and Works of Horace Mann, Volume IV.* Boston: Lee and Shepart, 1891, 251.
6. Peabody, Andrew. "The Relation of Public Schools to the Civil Government," *Unitarian Review,* 6 (July 1876), 24-39.
7. President's Commission on Higher Education. *Higher Education for American Democracy.* New York: Harper and Brothers, 1947, 27.
8. Sexton, Patricia Cayo. *Education and Income.* New York: Viking Press, 1969, 40.
9. Shaw, George Bernard. *The Doctor's Dilemma.* New York: Brentano's, 1928.

Reading in an Electronic Media Age

James B. Macdonald

IS OUR CULTURE PRIMARILY SHAPED BY OUR TECHNOLOGY?

One can argue with justification that the automobile was responsible for a shift in our puritan attitude toward sexual relationships. When the young gained the mobility and privateness afforded by the use of the automobiles, a whole series of new opportunities for sexual experience arose. There seems to be general agreement that our sexual mores have changed dramatically during this same period. The automobile certainly has been intricately involved as a factor in that change.

Nothing, one might argue, is so fundamental to a society as the way it structures sexual relationships and the patterns of sexual behavior it accepts. If technology, therefore, has forced a shift in so basic an attitudinal and behavioral pattern, it is reasonable to suggest that technology can produce change in any area of our culture.

This being the case, it appears reasonable to ask whether fundamental educational changes have and will occur in our culture when there are basic changes in the technology of communication.

Perhaps the best known person who has proposed that our electronic means of communication is changing our culture is McLuhan (5). He and his collaborators propose a number of startling possibilities.

The fundamental axiom of McLuhan is that "the medium is the massage." He asserts that any technology gradually creates a totally new human environment. Environments are active processes, not passive wrappings.

The fundamental change in the past thirty odd years has been from a "hot" linear type of communication to a "cool" pattern medium. Thus, the process by which messages are communicated is radically different when one shifts from a linear, written-word message to a multisensory participation in a pattern of electronic dots on television.

The written word has served civilization well. It was the basic way of communication that freed man from his tribal state of dependence upon oral traditions. It freed the individual to define himself as a separate person and to develop outside the context of the tribe. This type of communication has now run its course, and the electronic media as new extensions of man have carried us into a new culture.

McLuhan used the analogy of radar in the defense of cities. In the past, balloons were placed aloft to defend cities from attack. With the coming of radar, the balloons interfered with the detection of airplanes, and so a totally new approach to defense was developed. By implication, the development of television may not only become more prominent but may actually replace reading as the main way of communicating information in our culture.

Reading, if this analysis is accurate, will become an art form; for, as McLuhan suggests, the replaced technologies of the past are not competitive in the mainstream of information giving but are new art forms. Thus, if our culture is moving as is suggested, reading will not disappear but will take on a new function in the culture as an art form.

The major resistance to accepting this viewpoint of our changing culture is our perspective on content. The linear reading media place their emphasis upon the message being carried. Thus, the content is the focal point. This situation makes it hot in the sense that the intended meaning does not allow for as much reader participation in its creation. There is, relatively speaking, only one meaning intended.

As powerful as this technique has been, it has not been clearly recognized that the medium—i.e., the process of communication—carries a message also. Seldes (7) comments that one common criticism is that TV, movies, and radio can't be substitutes for textbooks. Seldes suggests the same struggle took place when printed books for students replaced the oral authority of the teacher. "Any institution that lasts a long time creates vested interests, and people who benefit by it are inclined to protect the institution as a way of protecting themselves."

Print made illiterates inferior and gave rise to the new discipline of learning to read. Electronics are again changing the culture and producing new disciples:

Print	Electronics
1. Requires ability to read	1. No special training involved
2. Usually experienced individually	2. Usually experienced in company
3. Taken in small doses	3. Taken in large doses
4. Relatively slow diffusion	4. Very rapid diffusion
5. Can be reread and checked	5. Generally can't be reobserved
6. Inexpensive to produce, expensive to consume	6. Expensive to produce, cheap to consume
7. Created for minorities	7. Created for majorities

One may easily see the spirit of a new age in the preceding comparison. This new age has some of the democratic communal and participatory overtones of elements of the youth culture of today.

Carpenter (2) talks about the new media as new languages. He feels that print (and then reading) was the completion of a process of linear expression begun with the oral but frozen with the introduction of the alphabet. "Events were arranged chronologically and hence, it was assumed, causally; relationship, not being, was valued. The author became an *authority*; his data were serious, that is, *serially* organized. Such data, if sequentially ordered and printed, conveyed value and truth; arranged any other way, they were suspect."

The new electronic language is not this way. Television, for example, is an immediate pattern or whole which presents multisensory stimuli in a combination of language, music, art, and dance. In other words, TV presents a message that print does not (as does print present a unique one). There is no way that the same message can be carried over different media.

As Carpenter says, "The problem has been falsely seen as democracy vs. the mass media. But the mass media are democracy. The book itself was the first mechanical mass medium. What is being asked, of course, is: Can books' monopoly of knowledge survive the challenge of the new languages? The answer is "No." What should be asked is "What can print do better than any other medium and is that worth doing?"

At present we do not know what the printing media can do best. What we do know is that reading as an activity is rapidly becoming less important in our culture.

The defense of teaching reading is best made in terms of further school work which necessitates being able to read; that is, as long as the school insists upon structuring its curricular tasks in forms which are predominantly dependent upon learners being able to read the printed word at a fairly sophisticated level of skill, then reading as we know it would seem to be necessary.

It is, in the writer's opinion, an open question as to whether we need to structure our curricula these ways. His best guess is that we do not need to do it this way at all, that reading need not be nearly so important even for school work. The reason we probably keep going this way is the huge vested interest in maintaining the status quo found in the materials we possess and the strong press of vested interest in teaching methodology. Thus, what material would replace print, and what methodology would we use?

One area where we have data concerns the necessity of producing highly sophisticated and skilled people for the work force. An interesting book by Berg (1) examines data relevant to the relationship between what is learned in school and what the majority of students need to know to function in most jobs after graduation from high school. Berg finds little evidence of strong relationships between school learning and adequate functioning on the job.

Where reading appears to still provide a meaningful role is in the creation of functional abilities possessed by an educated elite of professionals, scientists, and managers who are a minority of our population. The use of school credentials by society beyond this possible one is based on factors other than the relationship of what is learned to what is needed for a job.

Some persons have charged that the reading culture and reading tasks in school are fundamentally at the service of a paternalistic power structure. Whether capitalistic or not, reading ability can be said to be a fundamental way of discriminating the middle and upper classes from lower classes and blacks. Correlation does not prove any causation, but a vicious pattern does exist in this regard.

In the writer's opinion it is indeed implicit in the position taken by Illich in *Deschooling Society* that the whole environment is educative and that we do not really need schools as we know them to educate persons adequately but that schools are the pivotal link in a system which tends to oppress the majority of people. Of course, the media of print are the major media of the schools.

EDUCATION OR ENTERTAINMENT?

With the advent of mass media the total environment has again become as educational as it was prior to the age of print. The sheer quantity of information conveyed by press-magazines-TV-radio far exceeds that conveyed by texts and instruction in schools. Thus, the monopoly of the book has been broken and with it the very basic needs and premises of schooling. Educators have tended to respond to this threat by viewing new media as entertainment rather than education. To the student of media this trend is patent nonsense.

The problem arises because the print culture does not compete well with the new media culture. Any number of studies reveal that children watch TV often and prefer it to reading. Thus, the linear skill learning for a print culture that takes place in schools is not competitive for the young's time and interest unless such activity is imposed.

It is this fact that makes compulsory education a different matter than it was prior to World War II. It is not just a matter of compelling the young to attend but of compelling them to spend their time and effort in a print culture when they no longer prefer to operate in that realm. Thus, new media cannot be written off as entertainment. The question may well be whether reading is not becoming simple entertainment rather than the reverse.

ONE BROADER EDUCATIONAL ISSUE

There are considerable concern and discussion at the present time about the use of behavioral objectives in schooling. The idea, though around for quite a spell, has become embodied in guidelines for many federal and state financed programs and is being thrust upon many school systems as a vehicle for curriculum development (including reading programs).

The behavioral objectives approach is a good example of the fruition and, indeed, culmination of the print mentality in operation. Thus, the same linear, "hot" message is programed in light of the media. That is, the control is stated in behavioral terms, and the situation in which the behavior should occur is specified. Thus, the hot goal (specific behavior) and the media (i.e., behavior-in-situation) are specified. Since behavioral objectives are written, they take on the aura of authority; and the serial nature (sequential step programing) of their organization puts them in the print media mentality.

Seen in this light, behavioral objectives are the epitome and perhaps the last gasp of a passing (in predominance) cultural media (i.e., print). It is doubtful that under these circumstances behavioral objectives can be helpful in the long run, and they may well represent a disastrous delaying tactic in facing up educationally to the meaning of our new electronic media age.

COLLABORATIVE RELATIONSHIPS AMONG MEDIA?

Assuming that we are in a transitional stage between a print culture and an electronic media culture, there are many questions and problems which have arisen concerning the relationship and reinforcement of different media with one another. Although a McLuhan would surely argue that print and TV are radically different, we have seen the development of at least two major examples on TV—*Sesame Street* and *The Electric Company*—which are oriented toward facilitating children's reading and number work through TV. *Sesame Street*, for example, may well teach many of the twelve million three-, four-, and five-year-olds in the United States to count to ten and to recite the alphabet. But is this instruction its major educational function? And what of those youngsters who would have come to school with these skills anyway?

The case is not clear. We simply do not know how much of a facilitator TV can be for learning to read, nor do we know what the ideal relationships of these two media are to each other. What is clear is that print media cannot ignore TV and that to solve the problem of educational TV research is needed to find out whether the two media are mutually exclusive or collaborative in their potential for learning.

Schramm and Chu (6) summarize what research says in this area. The results are not too helpful. Generally speaking, there are no significant differences when youngsters are taught by TV or conventional methods. The researchers suggest that these findings mean ". . . that television can do its part in this combination, and one goal of future research is to find what combinations will be more efficient than either classroom teaching or television teaching alone."

NEW ROLE FOR THE READING TEACHER?

It seems inevitable that the teaching of reading and/or the reading teacher must become part of a larger function and concern in the coming years. The concern will be for learning to communicate in all prevalent media, not just through the printed word. Teachers will have to become much less parochial in their concerns and much more broadly concerned and talented in other media.

Thus, there are already and will continue to be increasing needs for the young to have experience with and to be able to analyze and to criticize what is going on in the different media in our culture. Reading and language arts, which are strictly print oriented, will need to move over and develop into media-oriented studies which involve the young with know-how in TV, radio, and films as well as print.

As Culkin (3) says, "The child lives totally immersed in a visual culture, and yet there is not one-half of one percent of the elementary schools in the United States which spend one hour a week helping him to interpret and to become selective and discriminating about visual stimuli." It is this interpretation, selection, and discrimination that will help the child "read" the new media and toward which the school and the reading teacher must be oriented.

This goal means a further broadening of what still might be called a language experience approach to reading. Only now the experience must go beyond experience in the oral and print culture alone and must deal with the new media as languages by responding to our new visual culture, and most specifically to television (4).

In a rather interesting way the new media may change the instructional process in ways that progressive educators would approve of. Certainly the consideration of the whole environment as educative, the role of increased participation on the part of learners (cool media), and the concern for the total person as his whole experience impinges on him are cornerstones of the progressive era. Perhaps television will do for progressive educational ideas what couldn't be done by reason alone. Thus, there is a case for predicting that the new visual cultural technology will change our practices whether we will it or not.

SCIENCE FICTION AND/OR THE FUTURE?

Perhaps the best way to put electronic media and print into perspective does not rest in the present uses of electronic media but in their potential development. Print (and reading) other than speed reading (techniques) would seem to have developed to their logical finished forms—but not so with electronic media.

Although speculation is always risky, there is no doubt that electronic media can soon become a two-way and not simply a one-way reception. With this development may also come a variety of ways of receiving through simulated sensory input beyond eyes and ears. Thus, the brave new world of the "feelies" may not be far in the future.

The point here is that electronic media are in their infancy. We do not know what will develop; we know only the general directions the media will take. It seems justifiable to suggest that the need for print and reading, now under heavy attack as major sources of information, will diminish even more as newer media developments emerge.

Reading in an Electronic Media Age

References

1. Berg, Ivar. *Education and Jobs: The Great Training Robbery.* Boston: Beacon Press, 1969.
2. Carpenter, Edmund. "The New Languages," *Explorations in Communication* by Marshall McLuhan and Edmund Carpenter. Boston: Beacon Press, 1960, 162-179.
3. Culkin, John. "Tomorrow's Programs for Children: Who? What? and Where?" *Action for Children's Television,* prepared by Evelyn Sarson. New York: Avon Books, 22.
4. Gattegno, Caleb. *Towards a Visual Culture.* New York: Avon Books, 1969.
5. McLuhan, Marshall. *Understanding Media.* New York: McGraw-Hill, 1964.
6. Schramm, Wilbur, and Godwin C. Chu. *Learning from Television.* Washington, D.C.: National Association of Educational Broadcasters, 1967.
7. Seldes, Gilbert. "Communication Revolution," *Explorations in Communication* by Marshall McLuhan and Edmund Carpenter. Boston: Beacon Press, 1960, 196-199.

The Reading Establishment and Teacher Education

Wayne Berridge

Demands for the reading establishment to do something about improving children's chances for success in learning to read are perhaps greater today than at any time before. Yesterday we were concerned that three or four pupils in each class were achieving at several grade levels below the expected grade placement. Today we are confronted with massive failure in which whole urban school populations are showing substantially depressed achievement.

The assumption made in the past was that the placement of a specially trained reading person within a school or district would provide the means of combating difficulties children might experience in learning to read. This was a valid assumption when reading problems were essentially limited to three or four students per class. Given today's reading scene in the urban setting with the concurrent social, economic, and political problems, this position is no longer tenable.

What type of trained reading personnel do we need in the public schools? Do we need highly trained specialists? Can we define the role and the preparation requirements for such specialists?

How relevant are existing practices of teacher education institutions, state certification requirements, and statements of guidelines for preparing reading specialists made by such organizations as the International Reading Association?

In this paper, I would like to explore some of the underlying assumptions for the preparation of reading specialists and their role at the public school level. To facilitate this discussion, several areas are examined: 1) current practices in preparing various levels of reading specialists, 2) the assumptions on which reading specialists operate within the school system, 3) the relationship of the "reading establishment" to the concept of reading specialists, and 4) suggested alternatives to the present system of preparing trained personnel.

Presently the preparation of reading education personnel for the schools focuses on the training of reading specialists. Usually the reading specialists receive this training at the graduate level; sometimes as part of the requirement for a master's degree program. Such programs prepare reading specialists to perform a variety of duties within the school reading program. In practice, the role of the reading specialist has been that of a remedial reading teacher, a diagnostician, an inservice programer, or an administrator or coordinator of reading programs.

The Professional Standards and Ethics Committee of the International Reading Association has defined a hierarchy of roles based on duties performed by the reading specialist (*15*):

Special Teacher of Reading

A Special Teacher of Reading has major responsibility for remedial and corrective and/or developmental reading instruction.

Reading Clinician

A Reading Clinician provides diagnosis, remediation, or the planning of remediation for the more complex and severe reading disability cases.

Reading Consultant

A Reading Consultant works directly with teachers, administrators, and other professionals within a school to develop and implement the reading program under the direction of a supervisor with special training in reading.

Reading Supervisor (Coordinator or Director)

A Reading Supervisor provides leadership in all phases of the reading program in a school system.

Specific areas to be covered in programs preparing reading specialists are suggested. Common to all levels of preparation of reading specialists is the recommendation that the sequence include a course in diagnosis and correction of reading disabilities and a course in clinical or laboratory practicum in reading. At many colleges and universities, these two courses represent the heart of the master's program in reading. Those reading specialists who expect to work with remedial reading students are encouraged to take additional courses in diagnosis and remediation and practicum work.

From the foregoing description of the preparation of reading specialists, it is apparent that learning to diagnose and remediate reading difficulties of children plays a major role in preparing the reading specialist for work in the schools. This basic premise is a sound one. That the reading specialists should find out why Johnny can't read and take steps to alter conditions so Johnny can read cannot be questioned. What can be questioned is the assumptions underlying diagnostic and remedial techniques, the way these techniques are carried out, and the staff level at which current practices are focused.

The suggested course requirements for all levels of preparation of reading specialists fail to mention relevant areas of study, such as, linguistics, cultural and social foundations, dialectical differences, and teaching children whose first language is other than English. Suggested courses emphasize the cognitive domain to the exclusion of affective factors, such as, utilizing various reflective, creative thinking activities and group discussion techniques.

UNDERLYING ASSUMPTIONS

It is not the purpose of this paper to question the sincerity of those people in the reading establishment who are engaged in the activities of reading specialists in the schools. It is, however, the purpose to critically examine some of the reasons why the role of the reading specialist needs reassessment.

The literature dealing with reading diagnosis and remediation has been to a great extent an exposition of particular approaches or programs with rather inconclusive research results as to the efficacy of any particular method. The diagnostic process has not been extensively examined (*17*). The most that can be said is that a variety of remedial reading strategies works under a variety of conditions. A more fruitful approach may be to critically analyze the underlying social assumptions as embodied in current practices of reading specialists.

Before dealing with the social issues involved, it is necessary to explore several factors relating to current practices of reading specialists. These factors are, in the opinion of the writer, directly related to the underlying social issues.

The first of these factors deals with current practices in staffing. As was noted earlier, reading specialists assume a number of duties within a school system. These duties performed by reading personnel can be divided into two categories: those who work directly with children as special reading teachers or clinicians and those who work directly with teachers or administrators as consultants or program coordinators and supervisors.

A current trend is to provide a reading resource teacher for one or more buildings. This person works directly with teachers on an inservice basis. Regardless of the role of the reading specialists, certain basic assumptions must be questioned concerning present staffing practices.

Certainly inservice needs exist. New teachers need orientation to reading programs and instructional resources that supervisory reading personnel can provide. The need exists to update classroom practices for more experienced faculty. The question that must be asked is how practical is it to assume that students' needs are being met by employing one reading person with thirty hours of reading education and related preparation while the thirty other teachers in the building may not have collectively thirty hours of reading education credits?

There are teacher education institutions that prepare reading specialists well, and there are schools that employ these reading specialists to advantage. The basic question remains, where should the emphasis fall in the preparation of reading personnel—inservice or preservice? It may be that the tremendous inservice needs in reading education cannot be met until a much stronger emphasis is placed on the preparation of reading personnel at the preservice level. Such an emphasis, however, should not ignore inservice needs which are the result of continued educational growth for classroom teachers. The dilemma facing the reading establishment is how to meet inservice needs of schools by preparing reading specialists and at the same time to provide preservice reading education that will, to a great extent, eliminate, modify, and redefine the role of the reading specialist at the inservice level.

Failure of the reading establishment to meet preservice reading education needs will result only in perpetuating the illusion that we are doing something about children's reading problems when in reality we will have become dependent upon these reading problems to support an industry of remedial reading.

It is the assertion of the writer that the reading establishment has given lip service to Austin's recommendations (2) for the preparation of preservice teachers but for political reasons has continued to focus on the reading specialist rather than the preparation of the classroom teacher to teach reading. One reason for this condition is the reading establishment's entanglement in compensatory education. This concept is developed further in a following section.

A second factor requiring further explication is the diagnostic process. The major rationale for any diagnosis is that there is something wrong with the child's learning and that if a diagnosis is carried out, the results will lead to prescriptive remediation.

Bateman (4) succinctly summarizes the underlying issues concerning the individual diagnostic approach.

1. To what extent are reading disabilities preventable by more adequate initial instruction? Today's assumption is that the child requires diagnosis; tomorrow's assumption may be that the reading program and teaching strategies should be diagnosed.

2. How effective is individually planned remediation versus other kinds of instruction? For example the apparent success of high school tutors (who are themselves poor readers) with young disabled readers must give us pause.

3. How much of the data obtained in given diagnostic procedures is actually used in a) remedial planning, b) basic research, c) parent counseling, and d) others?

4. How economical is the diagnostic-remedial approach compared to other strategies, including no treatment? Cost analyses might reveal startling differences as measured in cost per unit of reading gained.

5. If the diagnostic-remedial approach is found valid, what then is the relationship between diagnosis and remediation?

As an alternative strategy to individual diagnosis, Bateman suggests a model

of behavioral assessment which avoids technical jargon, utilizes criterion refer-
enced tests, and focuses on program and teaching deficiencies as opposed to
looking for deficiencies within the child (4).

There is a danger in becoming overreliant upon diagnostic-type decisions
when these decisions are based on a fixed-ability hypothesis. Such an assumption
attributes lack of achievement to a deficit in the child. The child, consequently,
becomes labeled, and teacher expectancies for the child's achievement develop
and are communicated to the child. An example of this is the practice of using
reading expectancy formulas to estimate a child's potential reading level.

It just may be that consciously or unconsciously the reading establishment
has encouraged a bit of mystique concerning the importance of reading diagnosis, perhaps implying that only highly trained personnel can deal with reading
problems. Indeed, the reason given by the IRA in establishing standards is based
on this concept.

> Reading is a complex process that develops within an individual through-
> out years of formal schooling and adult life. As a result of expanded
> knowledge, the demand for trained personnel in reading at all levels has
> increased tremendously. With the demand high and the supply short, the
> danger of unqualified persons attempting those tasks which only a trained
> reading specialist should undertake has become a very real one. One means
> of preventing such occurrences is by establishing minimum standards for
> the professional training of reading specialists (15).

Such proclamations have the effect of placing reading specialists on a pedestal
and placing the role of the reading specialist above mere mortals such as classroom teachers and children.

Now just what those tasks are that only a trained reading specialist can
perform is open to debate.

Children can learn from one another. Robertson (14) reports that when low
achieving fifth graders tutored first graders in reading, both groups improved. In
addition, fifth graders developed more positive attitudes toward reading and
school. It would be naive to argue that fifth graders acting as intergrade tutors
working with first grade pupils could make the same instructional decisions that
a reading specialist could in similar circumstances. It would be equally naive to
assume that the classroom teacher is restricted to the technician level of decision
making (recipe teaching with a basal reader teacher's manual). Indeed, there are
probably few tasks now performed by reading specialists that classroom teachers
could not learn to cope with. What is stopping the classroom teacher is not only
a lack of reading education background but also the mystique of the reading
specialist. The reading specialist's relationship to the classroom teacher is a paternalistic relationship. The classroom teacher has learned to depend on the reading
specialist for diagnostic decisions.

The statement ". . . the danger of unqualified persons attempting those tasks
which only a trained reading specialist should undertake . . ." (15) is not designed to protect little children but rather to scare away scab labor from the
reading specialist market. After all, if the reading establishment is really con-

cerned with untrained persons teaching reading, why not first examine the class-room teachers' preparation?

THE READING ESTABLISHMENT AND THE READING SPECIALIST

The relationship between the reading establishment and the reading specialist is, according to this writer, as much political as it is professional in nature. The political aspect of this relationship is characterized by lobbying by state reading associations to provide money to school districts for hiring special teachers of reading. This action in a sense is a type of featherbedding by the reading estab-lishment. It might be more meaningful educationally to lobby for monies for school districts to pay inservice costs of preparing classroom teachers to teach reading.

A major social issue confronting the reading establishment today is the degree to which remedial reading programs are in effect compensatory programs. Com-pensatory programs are suspect because most of them fail (13). Compensatory programs are premised on the concept that something is missing and that this deficit can be compensated for by educational strategies. Compensatory pro-grams are not new to the American educational scene. As early as the end of the eighteenth century the public school system of Salem, Massachusetts, was offer-ing a free remedial reading class for poor children (8). (Incidentally, it wasn't any more successful than contemporary programs.)

Farber and Lewis (8) examine some of the assumptions underlying compen-satory educational programs:

It is one thing to recognize that the surplus population is hampered by learning problems—quite obviously the poor do have such problems in great numbers—but it is quite another to attribute these problems to a cultural background presumed to be *deprived*. It is one thing to place the learning problems of the surplus population in the context of externally imposed constraints—and another to isolate these learning problems, to approach them as though they are the only factors inhibiting the disadvan-taged poor from participating fully in the mainstream of American life. By doing so, we neglect all those conditions which must be remedied before the learning problems can be solved. No matter how technically proficient, no curriculum or pedagogical innovation will have very much impact upon a sick or hungry child whose daily struggle for existence cannot but alien-ate him from the public culture and those who give their allegiance to it. By isolating learning problems from their context we must invariably fail to confront the conditions of inequality which make victims of the dis-advantaged poor—but isolate them we do and, sociologically speaking, for understandable reasons.

The most damning statements these writers make against compensatory educa-tional strategies are that we have created an illusion of helping the disadvan-taged. Furthermore, safe in our illusion that we are actually helping the disad-vantaged, we have come to depend upon them as an industry.

An analogy between compensatory programs and reading programs can be made at two levels. First, the present staffing policy of utilizing reading specialists as a means of combating reading problems in the schools produces an illusion that we are doing something to solve the problem. This is not to say that reading specialists at the school level fail to perform useful functions. Specialists do help children overcome reading problems. Too often, however, specialists are spread too thin and assigned overwhelming case loads or inservice tasks. The point to be made is this: The present schools keep on producing reading failures. At best, the reading specialist may find himself propping up a system programed for failure.

An analogy can also be made on a broader scale. We cannot continue to operate on the basis that we can solve reading problems with a simple programatic approach without considering the broader community ramifications. "Believing as we do in the viability of its basic assumptions [compensatory education], failure is taken to mean that we have not yet found the right technique or program" (8). The community will not forever accept the onus of failure that compensatory reading programs imply. Recent militancy by minority groups is indicative of resistance to conventional educational reform. Minority parents want their children to learn to read. When published test scores of urban schools indicate failures, voices are raised in protest.

A recent article in the *Milwaukee Journal* (12) describes a confrontation between parents and school officials over published test scores:

> ...a member of the neighborhood council said special programs initiated to combat learning handicaps in inner city schools were apparently not working, as evidenced by low achievement scores.

"We have been programed to death, and what we're looking for is results."

SUGGESTED ALTERNATIVES

The major area of concern for the preparation of reading specialists should be that of preparing classroom teachers who are specialists at teaching reading in the classroom. This recommendation is logical in the light of the present oversupply of classroom teachers. An extended program including a fifth year for classroom teacher preparation would delay entry into the marketplace and allow a more intensive programing (19). This suggestion is premised on the assumption that the classroom teacher, given the preparation and allowed to assume the responsibility, can make meaningful diagnostic and evaluative decisions concerning the instructional program.

Yarington (18) describes a program that was implemented at the University of Massachusetts. Undergraduates were allowed to select reading education courses previously limited to graduate enrollment and thus acquired reading specialist competencies. In addition, the reading education courses were competency based and modularized to provide greater relevancy and flexibility in meeting specific needs.

What specifically should the competencies of the classroom reading specialist be? Present conditions indicate that we need personnel with a knowledge and an appreciation of cultural and language differences characteristic of urban student populations (3).

If reading teachers are to work effectively with black children, teachers must understand black dialect and black culture and adapt their teaching strategies accordingly. Teachers must study black culture and black dialect with sympathetic recognition of these factors as part of a legitimate minority culture (9). The child from the home where Spanish is spoken deserves similar consideration.

Further exploration of the urban child's language in relationship to his school, culture, and peer groups promises to provide useful insights for developing instructional strategies. What needs to be stressed is that the child's language and culture are not inferior but different (3, 11).

Basic classes of diagnosis and remediation that have traditionally been the heart of master's programs preparing reading specialists require reassessment. Alternatives to the time-consuming traditional, diagnostic approach need to be considered. One approach that could be explored is the behavior assessment techniques suggested by Bateman (4). Strategies that allow teachers to assess teaching techniques as well as pupil-learning outcomes represent another alternative.

Carroll (6) has formulated a model of school learning which stresses a criterion-referenced approach in which time is not treated as a fixed variable but allowed to vary according to the individual learner's needs. Such an approach allows an individual to progress at a meaningful rate without the stigma of failure.

A more pragmatic approach to the use of intelligence test results is in order. Instructional decisions based on IQ scores are more of a labeling process than a corrective procedure. This dependency on testing reflects the educational establishment's preoccupation with the fixed-ability hypothesis that in effect determines who can be educated. It is well to keep in mind that Binet never regarded the construct of intelligence as being of a static nature (16). Overdependence on standardized test results should be replaced with teacher attitudes that foster a healthy learning expectancy for all children.

Procedures which treat reading problems as child centered should be replaced with techniques which explore the relationship between the child and the school environment (10).

Preparation of reading personnel should include human relation workshops and techniques for enhancing a more humanistic classroom environment. One such strategy that might be explored is values clarification techniques (1).

Different models of learning need to be explored. As the school environment evolves toward less structure and more openness, the models of formal learning may need to be replaced with models of incidental learning. Such models would have the advantage of minimizing the social caste system of existing classrooms. The fear of failure is replaced by freedom to fail in order to further explore learning alternatives (5).

Reading personnel must be committed to community improvement. "Those who teach must not isolate their pedagogy from the political efforts of the surplus poor to reform those conditions which victimize them" (8).

Last, the "classroom reading specialist" needs to focus on the relevant problems at hand. Dennison (7) summarizes this position in his statement concerning Jose, a boy with a reading problem. "Jose's reading problem is Jose. Or to put it another way, there is no such thing as a reading problem. Jose hates books, schools, and teachers, and among a hundred other insufficiencies—all of a piece—he cannot read. Is this a reading problem?"

References

1. Abramowitz, Mildred W., and Claudia Macari. "Values Clarification in Junior High School," *Educational Leadership,* 29 (April 1972), 621-626.
2. Austin, Mary C., and Coleman Morrison. *The First R: The Harvard Report on Reading in Elementary School.* New York: Macmillan, 1963.
3. Baratz, Stephen S., and Joan C. Baratz. "Early Childhood Intervention: The Social Science Base of Institutional Racism," *Harvard Educational Review,* 40 (Winter 1970), 29-50.
4. Bateman, Barbara. "The Role of Individual Diagnosis in Remedial Planning for Reading Disorders," in E. O. Calkins (Ed.), *Reading Forum,* NINDS Monograph No. 11. Washington, D.C. 1971.
5. Brookover, Wilbur, and Edsel L. Erickson. *Society Schools and Learning.* Boston: Allyn and Bacon, 1969.
6. Carroll, John B. "A Model of School Learning," *Teachers College Record,* 64 (1963), 723-733.
7. Dennison, George. *The Lives of Children: The Story of the First Street School.* New York: Random House, 1969.
8. Farber, Bernard, and Michael Lewis. "Compensatory Education and Social Justice," *Peabody Journal of Education,* 49 (January 1972), 85-96.
9. Johnson, Kenneth R., and Herbert D. Simons. "Black Children and Reading: What Teachers Need to Know," *Phi Delta Kappan,* 53 (January 1972), 288-290.
10. Labov, William. "Academic Ignorance and Black Intelligence," *Atlantic Monthly,* 229 (June 1972), 59-67.
11. Labov, William, and Clarence Robins. "A Note on the Relation of Reading Failure to Peer Group Status in Urban Ghettos," *Teachers College Record,* 70 (1969), 395-399.
12. "Parents, Schools Argue about CORE ," *Milwaukee Journal,* May 4, 1972.
13. Riessmann, Frank. "Can Schools Teach Children: What Is Stopping Them— What Is to Be Done?" *Journal of Educational Research and Development,* 5 (Winter 1972), 83-90.
14. Robertson, Douglas J. "Intergrade Tutoring: Children Learn from Children," in Sam Leaton Sebesta and Carl J. Wallen (Eds.), *The First R: Readings on Teaching Reading.* Chicago: SRA, 1972.
15. "Roles, Responsibilities, and Qualifications of Reading Specialists," *Journal of Reading,* 12 (October 1968), 60-63.
16. Schwebel, Milton. *Who Can Be Educated?* New York: Grove Press, 1968.
17. Strang, Ruth. *Reading Diagnosis and Remediation.* Newark, Delaware: International Reading Association, 1968.

18. Yarington, David J. "A Performance Curriculum for Training Reading Teachers," *Journal of Reading,* 13 (October 1969), 21-24.

19. Zedler, Empress Y. "Development of Competencies for the Teaching of Reading to Children Who Have Not Learned under Conventional Procedures," in E. O. Calkins (Ed.), *Reading Forum,* NINDS Monograph No. 11. Washington, D.C., 1971.

Reading, Bureaucracy, and Individual Adaptation

Will Roy

This paper is not really about reading, nor is it about bureaucracies; it is about how individuals adapt to a bureaucratic structure and about what happens to the teaching and learning of reading because of the selected adaptation. Let us first discuss some basic assumptions.

SCHOOLS ARE BUREAUCRATIC IN NATURE

Rogers (*17*) calls education "... rigid, outdated, bureaucratic, and incompetent." Bloomberg (*4*) sees schools as factories, and Katz (*11*) says that education is based on a nineteenth century bureaucratic model. Bidwell (*3*) details quite well how schools compare to the bureaucratic model, and even the uninitiated reader of Weber will clearly see how school systems reflect his characteristics of bureaucracy. To illustrate, there are fixed functions with rules governing those functions; persons are placed in a hierarchical structure; and positions are given on the basis of supposed expertise (*8*). It seems unnecessary to "prove" it again in this paper, unless you are like the Vermonter who says, "Everybody knows what's going on, but we read the papers anyway to see who got caught at it!" Believe me, the schools have been caught at it!

A PRIMARY GOAL OF BUREAUCRACIES IS EFFICIENCY

It is apparent that this statement is true. Business is meant to be discharged objectively; no personal element is to halt the machinery. Bureaucratic organizations have been advanced because of their technical superiority over other forms of organizations. It is the advantage of the machine over hand labor. Bureaucracies are meant not only to be more precise in accomplishing tasks but also to be cheaper (8).

THAT STUDENTS LEARN TO READ IS A PRIMARY GOAL

It is assumed that even if you would advance more idealistic goals, you will agree that this is a real goal of the school. When we realize how easily parents become agitated over the disclosure of reading test scores and how much money—federal and local—is spent for the express purpose of achieving this goal, we get an indication of the high priority given to reading. Finally, it is not difficult to convince anyone of the need for reading skills if a child is simply to continue his schooling "successfully," as that phenomenon now occurs.

ALTHOUGH BUREAUCRACIES, SCHOOLS ARE NOT VERY EFFICIENT

If schools were efficient, would there be need for an annual IRA get-together? It seems to me that those who attend come for one of four basic reasons: 1) to commiserate with one another over failures, 2) to brag about some recent success, 3) to search for new techniques and knowledge, or 4) to meet old friends and make new ones.

This lack of efficiency in bureaucracies is referred to by Merton (13) as its dysfunction. In schools, for example, control over the clients often displaces educational goals (23). Often what are considered the means (rules, procedures) to an end become the actual ends—". . . an instrumental value becomes a terminal value" (13).

TEACHERS AND STUDENTS ADAPT DIFFERENTLY

Obviously, if we all reacted the same way to bureaucracies, we wouldn't have to argue about them. Bureaucracies do force us to adapt, but that adaptation is not always one of social anomie (social disintegration and alienation) as Arnstine (2) argues. Anomie, nevertheless, is a major unintended consequence of bureaucracy and should be explained further.

ANOMIE

For the famed sociologist, Durkheim the anomic society is one in which "there ceases to be clear norms of behavior" (20). Merton (13) argues that the norms are clear enough but that the behaviors they allow do not permit most people to realize the societal goals. In Merton's conception, there are both culturally defined goals—purposes and interests which are held as legitimate objectives for all members of society—and culturally defined means which explain, regulate, and control the acceptable modes of reaching out for the prevailing goals. As long as people derive satisfaction from both values—the end and the means—there is equilibrium. Anomie results when either the goals or the means or both are rejected.

PATTERNS OF ADAPTATION

Returning to the societal institution which interests us, we can see that schools have goals (e.g., the teaching of reading) and institutionalized means for accomplishing the goals (e.g., teaching guides, grouping). Although the means may vary among the schools, all members of each school recognize the legitimized means for performing their tasks. Moreover, the students realize what means are available for them to achieve the institutional goal.

What possible responses are open to us? It is possible to be satisfied with both the goals and the sanctioned means. We can accept the goal but find alternate routes for getting there, or we can accept the means without ever achieving the goal. We can reject both, or we can choose to change both by substituting others. Merton (13) presents the possibilities in the following typology:

MODES OF INDIVIDUAL ADAPTATION

		Cultural Goals	Institutionalized Means
I.	Conformity	Accepts	Accepts
II.	Innovation	Accepts	Rejects
III.	Ritualism	Rejects	Accepts
IV.	Retreatism	Rejects	Rejects
V.	Rebellion	Rejects/Accepts new values	Rejects/Accepts new values

Using the above typology provides us with an interesting way of looking at how we might respond to bureaucracies. Let us accept the proposition that teaching reading and learning to read are primary goals of schools. We can allow ourselves to be vague about the means. There is no need for us to enter "The Great Debate." We shall simply agree that the institutionalized means are those which are sanctioned by that particular school system in which one is employed and in which the student is served. As long as there are bureaucratically imposed means, it really doesn't make any difference what method is used in terms of this somewhat tentative analysis. Also, it is possible and probable that any individual can adapt at different times in different ways. One of the following patterns emerges, however, as the dominant pattern at a given time.

THE CONFORMING PATTERN OF ADAPTATION

According to Merton (13), to the extent that a society is stable the conformist pattern is the most common. It should be expected, then, that this is the dominant adaptation occurring in most schools. Without a great deal of conformity, the school is in constant turmoil.

Those that agree with the value placed on reading and the means used by the school to achieve that goal are adapting in a conforming way. Teachers have a need to be a part of the school (12). They accept, at least in a traditional setting, the reward-punishment model, competition, the giving of grades, testing, and the need for efficiency and for preserving the system in which they are participating. Teachers are not to be confused with the ritualist (although the danger exists that they can shift to that pattern) because they really believe in the goal and think that it can be achieved given the methods at their disposal. They evidently have enough success to continue the way they are. Our purpose here is not to argue whether the correlation between the goal and means actually exists.

It must be apparent that many children share these values with their teachers. One needs only watch children play reading teacher. In most cases the children's initiative behavior is not satire but reflects an agreement with the means for teaching reading and a belief in reading as a goal. There are, after all, some students in school who really enjoy reading! The conforming children have learned the game and have agreed with the rules. In a traditional setting, they are "A" seekers, praise hunters, punishment avoiders, efficiency experts, and teacher pleasers.

Both the teachers and children find school acceptable. They do not complain but perform the tasks expected of them with the expectation that the goal will be reached. The teacher believes in the worth of what he is doing, and the child has learned to meet the teacher's expectations by presenting an intellectual image through reading well. That image is reinforced by test scores (24). When research is cited, it is to justify the operation the way it is (25). The community tends to respect these teachers and often points to this type child as a model for others.

THE INNOVATIVE PATTERN OF ADAPTATION

When the teacher has internalized the cultural value of reading but does not accept the means for achieving that end, he becomes an innovator. He may, for example, reject reading tests because he feels they are misused. He would rather follow Riessmann's advice to make positive assumptions about the ability of children to learn and push it to the limit (15). He may well be the subversive teacher, the militant, the supporter of student demands, but only in relation to means for achieving established goals. To illustrate, he may have been the teacher in a district who began to ask for different texts (e.g., books for and about Blacks).

On the positive end of the continuum, he searches for new ways to teach reading even if doing so involves some risks. On the negative end, he has so internalized the goal that he will use any means to accomplish the goal—including changing test scores! The goal becomes so important that any method is justified even if the possibility of harming the child exists. If reading scores could be improved by wiring the chairs with electricity, given the opportunity he would do it. He may even persist in a method with "guaranteed results" when parents, other teachers, and children respond negatively. I suspect that the more negative aspects of the behavior modification approach are caused by the adoption of this pattern of behavior.

The child who has internalized this goal but who does not subscribe to the means will react similarly. At one extreme, he cheats on tests and fakes his book reports; at the other, he reads on his own rather than conform to reading tasks which he considers unhelpful. He is either a good reader who bothers the teacher by reading too fast or the wrong books or he is the charmer who makes one believe that he can read. When he becomes an adult, he will have a library; but it will be to impress others with an assumed reading eagerness. Or, if he is a reader, he may have a library so esoteric as to be considered odd.

THE RITUALISTIC PATTERN OF ADAPTATION

When one rejects the goal but accepts the prescribed means, he is a ritualist. To have high hopes is to invite frustration; to lower the aspirations is to produce satisfaction and security. Adherence to rules and procedures, which are normally means, becomes an end (13). The ritualist can be compared to a rain dancer who does his dance step by step without ever knowing for sure if there is any connection between the ritual and rain (24). He is the person for whom the word "bureaucrat" has become a derogatory epithet.

It is possible that because he feels guilty about his own lack of reading, he pushes children to read more (24). He calls reading a pleasure, but he makes it work. As Wolcott points out, the reading class reflects a work ethic, but the sequence is reversed. Reading pleasure is followed by work—seat work, drill, and workbooks. Overall, he is the proponent of the "keep busy rule." He may relish the "ditto method" of teaching, and he is an advocate of the "Mount Everest Curriculum." He uses certain materials, texts, and methods because they are there. He is more concerned with classroom efficiency than individual learning rates, and he may well restrict the children from redoing things over which he has no direct control (6, 24). In terms of reading, he gives so many nonreading assignments and he talks so much that actual reading time is effectively lost (24).

It is relatively easy to explain how this phenomenon occurs in schools. A great emphasis on ability (especially in terms of job specialization) makes *what one can do* more important than *who one is*. "Thus the culture begins to reward relatively skin-surface materialistic characteristics" (1). In many school systems, it was found that principals and supervisors evaluated teachers on three highly visible characteristics: 1) the ability to control the social behavior of pupils, 2) the ability to make abundant and relevant bulletin boards, and 3) the ability to keep a good plan book (7). The system, then, causes the ritualistic behavior which may be only slightly related to good teaching practices.

A consequence of ritualistic behavior was demonstrated twelve years ago by the Project Talent study which showed that textbooks used by most high school seniors and freshmen were unsuitable for their reading abilities (*21*). When one further considers that the results were given as evidence for the promotion of individualizing instruction in the schools—and one looks for such programs—one easily becomes convinced of the stranglehold that ritualists have on the schools.

Perhaps the most observable result of ritualistic behavior is the custodial orientation of so many schools. The means originally devised to instruct are used simply to control. Control becomes the theme of the school (*23*). The ritualist is a close-minded person, and there is evidence to support that the close-minded person tends to be more custodial (*22*) and less receptive to innovation (*5*). The attitude and behavior evolve from a feeling of threat (*16*) and a realization that rewards are meted out for using that behavior (*7*). Students usually respond in kind.

For some children, the idea of being a reader is not very important. Due to a lack of early success, their becoming readers may even seem to be unattainable. Yet, they are willing to play the game. They insist on it. More than once the writer suggested to students, whom he was visiting when the teacher was absent, that they do something different, only to get the reply from many, "Oh no, at this time we get into our reading groups, and you have to listen to us." By submitting to their routine, the writer really had little to do. Strangely enough, although *they* were making the decisions, the ritual was the guideline. The children announced what was coming up at every turn. They even asked the writer to pass out the seat work. Many children are willing to submit to doing reading work, as Wolcott calls it, even though they don't become readers by so doing. The work sheet and the drill are ends in themselves. Children are so conditioned as to question very little; they accept our control mechanisms such as lining up, raising hands, and doing innocuous little tasks as part of schooling.

Put another way, this type of student is rigidly conforming, but he doesn't really know why. Like the ritualistic teacher, he has confused the means with the end.

THE RETREATIST PATTERN OF ADAPTATION

This pattern is perhaps the least common; for it does not include those people who leave the system but rather those who remain *in* the school but not *of* it. They have rejected both the value of knowing how to read and the means for achieving that goal. They have given up; they are the defeated ones.

The escaping teacher goes into "inhouse retreat." If he has sympathetic colleagues, he will create an informal group which will sanction his defense reactions, his apathy, his disinterest, and his lack of self-involvement (*1*). He sees no need to fool around with methods or curriculum because to do so is useless activity; and who cares anyway? He can be characterized by his laziness and remarks, such as, "Who can teach these kids anything?" He sees himself as invisible. He feels that he is not important to others—adults or children (*12*). He has been unable to succeed; and because of internalized prohibition, he cannot innovate. He, therefore, rejects both the goal and the means, but he substitutes nothing.

Silberman (*19*) argues that because a child cannot read, his attitude changes. The child may simply withdraw from what he considers to be competitive. If he doesn't substitute another goal or other means, he is retreating. He simply abandons all attempts. He likes large groups because he can find comfort in the fact that he is less likely to be called upon (*9*). He doesn't wish to participate. He sleeps or daydreams and simply tries to escape the requirements of the reading class. He is passive, but the passivity is destructive and unlike the passivity of many conformists which is seen by the teachers as being constructive.

THE REBELLIOUS PATTERN OF ADAPTATION

It is possible to reject the goal and the sanctioned means and to substitute another goal and other means. Merton (*13*) distinguishes between Scheler's concepts of "ressentiment" and rebellion. In the former, the feeling is of hate and envy—one condemns what he secretly craves. In the latter, the craving itself is condemned. There is allegiance to a new myth and a new group.

The rebel attempts to work from without the system because he perceives the reigning goals and means to be arbitrary. He is convinced neither of the necessity to be able to read nor of the means which are approved. He feels that the need to read is a myth and points to successful people who are not good readers and to ways of life which require little or no reading. He is a firm believer that other goals (e.g., life adjustment) are more worthwhile and that the emphasis on the teaching of reading is destructive. Needless to say, he is found most at universities and in alternative schools.

The rebellious child may not so easily opt to leave the system. So he does his rebelling somewhat differently, and he may end up being expelled from the system. Rather than achieving in reading, he may well view achievement as constituting doing things which upset the aims of the teacher and the school. Withdrawing, according to Silberman (*19*), can include clowning or rebelling. The small child who continually refuses to read while choosing to do another task is a rebel. The older child may actually demonstrate against an emphasis on reading work when it conflicts with furthering interests he considers more important. In any case, this is not an anomic pattern of behavior because other goals and means are substituted.

Because he deviates from the norms, the rebel is seen most often as an aggressive disrupter; he is seen as active destructive. However, it is possible that the child's rebellion is constructive behavior in terms of his own goals and means for achieving them. The behavior is as likely to be creative as it is to be destructive.

To the writer's knowledge this pattern was first introduced by Rawlin (*14*); and it is added to Merton's typology as another possible form of adaptation. Unlike the rebellious pattern which it may resemble, the censorious pattern is rather a form of conformity. Rawlin defines this pattern as one which seeks to safeguard the higher values of society. For example, the constitution sets forth a pluralistic ethic; yet, our goals and means are defined by a singular ethic—white, middle class Protestant values. For evidence, one need only be aware of the controversy surrounding reading texts.

The censorious teacher is neither a dropout nor a rebel. He works within the system to further the pluralistic ethic. He sees himself as rational and mature and living within the spirit of the constitution. He may well fight for the right to read, but he would also protect the right for not having to. Like many teachers he is placed in the position of identifying either with the child or with the school (*12*). He chooses the former. He deals with ideal values as opposed to the real values held by schoolmen. He asks that schools live up to their promise as democratic institutions. He demands that they live up to their stated philosophy (e.g., the uniqueness and worth of the individual). He sees as hypocritical that teachers who read only *Life* or *Reader's Digest* push children to read (*24*).

The censorious teacher is willing to be responsible for his actions and violates unjust regulations. As Schacht (*18*) puts it, "Civil disobedience manifests this form of principled rejection." Basically, it is a demand that we practice what we preach. If the school is a democratic institution, "Why," he asks, "is it characterized by authoritarianism? If we value creativity and critical thinking, why do we bore children by repetitious and boring tasks?" At the very least, he would ask that we live up to our supposed efficiency.

It is likely that the emergence of the censorious child is a more recent development. He is becoming more sophisticated in his dealings with the system. When a child reminds us that we are not living up to our stated ideals, he is adopting the censorious pattern. The student rights movement is certainly a good example. As students become more aware of the ideals we espouse, students are likely to react negatively to the real way we operate. Reading will no longer be reading work. If it is really a pleasure to read, students will demand that we make it pleasureful and that we at least demonstrate our own pleasure in the act. How many children, would you guess, have ever seen adults reading to one another in a circle? How many children have seen their teachers reading anything but the texts they are using in the classroom?

Someday, one of these children will ask, as Herndon (*10*) suggests, that we give them time to read instead of just time to practice reading.

THE EFFECT ON READING ACHIEVEMENT

A needed study might well be one in which children's modes of adaptation are compared to their achievements in reading. For that matter, assuming that it is teachers who adapt various patterns, does reading achievement vary in accordance to the adaptation of the teacher? While admitting to no hard data, the writer is willing to take some guesses which are hopefully consistent with the foregoing descriptions.

We must remember that in this paper conformity is not defined as behavior which results from external pressure. Rather, it is an acceptance of, an agreement with, and a belief in the goal and in the way of achieving it. Consequently, I can argue that such acceptance, agreement, and belief stem from teachers and students who are comfortable because they have experienced success. This type of teacher has the faith, expectations, and skills to help students achieve in reading. The conformist child is the average to better than average reader.

It is too difficult to predict outcomes for the innovative pattern of adaptation. It is possible that this type of teacher would excite and motivate children towards greater reading achievement. Yet, it is also possible for the teacher to frighten children and lead them to better reading through dictatorial methods. Since the goal is so highly valued, it is likely that reading achievement will improve under this teacher.

Although the innovative child may on occasion be a cheat or a faker, his acceptance of the value of reading will tend to provide him with the stimulus to become a good reader. These students are probably among the highest achievers, even though they don't do the work given them. Their grades reflect their not doing homework and the like rather than real achievement. When achievement test scores are looked at, teachers label these children as overachievers.

The ritualist teacher's concern with control and busy work may actually prevent students from achieving at their best. He produces average readers at best, and many would be below average. The ritualist child, confused as he is as to what reading is, does not achieve well in reading. His report card has a C or lower (if achievement in reading as opposed to completion of tasks is measured) and the comment: "He works very hard." This child is often graded on effort.

It is likely that the retreatist teacher is not only a failure but also a contributor to failure in his students. Since he doesn't care, it is difficult to see how the students will learn much during their tenure with him. Some students will learn in spite of him, of course. The lowest achiever in the classroom is obviously the retreatist child. He is our failure. He is often sent to remedial classes where he is given the opportunity to complete his withdrawal.

Since the truly rebellious teacher is not found within the school system, it is difficult to conjecture about his effect on reading achievement. It is possible, however, that his students would run the gamut. His class would be on a normal curve. Much would depend on the new emphasis given as a substitute goal. The rebellious child may also be positioned anywhere on a curve. He may very well be a good reader, but he doesn't value reading achievement over other goals. Consequently, he doesn't work at it. He could well be the child who gets an A for art or science but a D or F for reading.

It is the writer's guess that the censorious child fares very well in terms of reading achievement. He is probably at the top of his class, but he resents the "big to-do about it all." The writer also feels that the child who is in the hands of the censorious teacher will do well and become a better reader. He will do as well as the students with the conformist teacher, but the atmosphere will be more conducive to learning other things also. The threat of a single-minded emphasis will be removed, and the child will more easily choose a conformist or censorious pattern of adaptation.

CONCLUSIONS

Assuming that the various adaptations to bureaucracy exist and that we agree that some adaptations are undesirable, what can we do? Obviously, the anomic patterns (i.e. innovation, ritualism, and retreatism) are those with which we must be most concerned.

Notice that "innovation" as it is used here can be a negative as well as a positive way to adapt. At no time should reading become so important that any means will suffice. It is our duty to be censorious and to condemn practices which are contrary to more basic values. Harsh punishment, even if it leads to reading skills, cannot be tolerated. We must be careful not to place so much pressure on the teacher that he makes reading so important a goal as to lose sight of what he is doing to the child's well-being. Testing is one way by which we foster competition and allow some teachers and students to grasp at any means because it is justified by the end. We can't allow teachers to become coaches who win at any cost.

On the other hand, it is possible to allow the innovator the freedom to experiment with new methods. Of course, once we allow him this avenue, he is no longer in the anomic pattern. The institutionalized means are broad enough to include his innovation; and he is, therefore, in the conforming pattern. Rewarding innovation for innovation's sake (i.e., without relating it to the goal) will lead to ritualist behavior.

The ritualist is difficult to change. He must be made to see a relationship between means and ends. He should experience some success towards the goal. Giving him superior students might help, but it might also reinforce his beliefs about his routine. Under no circumstance should he any longer be rewarded for his ability to control children and to keep them busy but rather for his ability in advancing towards the goal. Consequently, supervisors and principals will have the responsibility of helping the ritualist identify the real purpose of his activities and of helping him to change that purpose.

Visitations to successful programs, inservice, and intensive follow up may be helpful in changing the ritualist towards believing that the desired goal is achievable. He will, however, need much support from his peers and his superiors. The difficulty we have, unfortunately, is that we really know so little about the relationship between the teaching act and learning.

For the child, our job is to relate activities so that he can understand that he is getting somewhere other than simply finishing a task. We must free him by offering and suggesting alternate routes. We have to be wary of routinizing his experience. Objectives should be made clear and explained rationally.

The temptation to recommend the firing of the retreatist teacher is overwhelming. But another bureaucracy, the teacher's union or association, protects him in order to preserve itself. If the retreatist cannot become involved and accept the goals and means and if he can't be fired, give him studyhall duty or promote him to the central office to handle duties like bus scheduling.

Involving the retreatist in group experiences with those who cherish and act upon the school's values might help move him along. You will, of course, have to provide the release time. Placing him in a team-teaching situation could pressure him to be involved. Like the ritualist, he must experience success, and he must be given the support by others. Involve him in decisions and hold him to his commitment.

Normal reaction is to ignore the retreatist child. We, therefore, must do the opposite. Influence his peers to work with him; offer him encouragement, and give him tasks at which he will succeed.

Since the rebel operates outside of the system, there is little you can do with him except to learn from him. Listen to him with an open mind. Visit his alternative school. Use what he has to say as a stimulus for the reexamination of the school's goals. Do the same listening to the rebel child. Negotiate with him. Hear his alternatives, suggest some, compromise, and let him make choices. Set limits only on completely undesirable behavior, but be clear as to why you are doing so. Give him some outlet doing what he values.

The censorius person causes little concern. We need him. We need people who can remind us when we are slipping. We need people with the courage to speak up and to act out their convictions. We must be wary not to confuse them with rebels. It is easy to perceive them that way. Consider the fate of Socrates or Christ.

FINAL STATEMENT

To worry about the method or the selection of texts is to tinker with change. Both simply reflect the norms of the bureaucracy; they do not create the norms. Thus, it is the bureaucracy that must be examined. The writer could recommend that the organizational structure of the school be changed, but to change the structure does not guarantee changes in behavior unless the change is radical and the people involved want it. We also know that changes, except minor ones, cannot be legislated. At one extreme we can "deschool" society; at the other, we can try to make bureaucracies work. Much doubt exists whether the latter is at all possible, and who really knows what will happen if we do the former.

The human relations approach may be a last-ditch effort to save the institutions as they exist. The writer would recommend that we at least try a shared-responsibility approach—that we get together, work together, and support one another in examining the patterns of bureaucracy—and that we ask the question Amy Lowell asked: "Christ! What are patterns for?"

References

1. Argyris, C. *Personality and Organization.* New York: Harper, 1957.
2. Arnstine, Donald. "Freedom and Bureaucracy in the Schools," in Vernon F. Haubrich (Ed.), *Freedom, Bureaucracy, and Schooling.* Washington, D.C.: Association for Supervision and Curriculum Development, NEA, 1971.
3. Bidwell, Charles. "The School as a Formal Organization," in J. C. Murch (Ed.), *Handbook of Organizations.* Chicago: Rand McNally, 1965.
4. Bloomberg, Warner. "The School as a Factory," paper prepared for the Interdistrict Institute, Homewood-Flossmoor, Illinois, mimeographed, 1967.
5. Bridges, Edwin M., and Larry B. Reynolds. *Administrator's Notebook,* 25 (February 1968).
6. Carlson, Richard O. *Adoption of Educational Innovation.* University of Oregon, Center for the Advanced Study of Educational Administration, 1965.
7. Eddy, Elizabeth M. *Becoming a Teacher.* New York: Teachers College, Columbia University, 1969.
8. Gerth, H. H., and C. Wright Mills (Eds. and Trans.). *Max Weber: Essays in Sociology.* London: Oxford University Press, 1946.
9. Guthrie, James W. "New Models: The Need for School Reform," in James W. Guthrie and Edward Wynne (Eds.), *New Models for American Education.* Englewood Cliffs, New Jersey: Prentice-Hall, 1971.
10. Herndon, James. *How to Survive in Your Native Land.* New York: Simon and Schuster, 1971.
11. Katz, Michael. *Class, Bureaucracy, and Schools: The Illusion of Educational Change in America.* Praeger, 1972.
12. Knoblock, Peter, and Arnold P. Goldstein. *The Lonely Teacher.* Boston: Allyn and Bacon, 1971.
13. Merton, Robert K. *Social Theory and Social Structure.* Glencoe, Illinois: Free Press, 1957.
14. Rawlin, John William, and Martin V. Shain (Eds.). *Drugs and Youth: Issues and Strategies—A Manual for Educators and Students.* Edwardsville, Illinois: Delinquency Study Project, Southern Illinois University, n.d.
15. Riessmann, Frank. *The Culturally Deprived Child.* New York: Harper and Row, 1962.
16. Rokeach, Milton. *The Open and Closed Mind.* New York: Basic Books, 1960.
17. Rogers, Carl. "Carl Rogers Says, 'It is My Observation. . . .' " *Newsletter,* Association for Humanistic Psychology, 7 (October 1970),1.
18. Schacht, Richard. *Alienation.* New York: Doubleday, 1970.
19. Silberman, Charles E. *Crisis in Black and White.* New York: Random House, 1964.
20. Simpson, George. *Emile Durkheim—Selections from His Work.* New York: Thomas Y. Crowell, 1963.
21. Tyler, Ralph W. (Ed.). *Educational Evaluation: New Roles, New Norms, 68th Yearbook.* Chicago: National Society for the Study of Education, 1969, 221-241.
22. Willower, Donald L., Terry L. Eidell, and Wayne K. Hoy. *The School and Pupil Control Ideology.* University Park: The Pennsylvania State University, 1967.

23. Willower, Donald L., and Ronald G. Jones. "Control in an Educational Organization" in James Raths, et al (Eds.), *Studying Teaching.* Englewood Cliffs, New Jersey: Prentice-Hall, 1967.
24. Wolcott, Harry F. "The Ideal World and the Real World of Reading: An Anthropological Perspective," mimeographed, 1968.
25. Wynne, Edward. "From Information to Reformation," in James W. Guthrie and Edward Wynne (Eds.), *New Models for American Education.* Englewood Cliffs, New Jersey: Prentice-Hall, 1971.

                                    Reading, Bureaucracy, and Individual Adaptation

Reading: The Impact of Classroom Interaction

John A. Zahorik

That the classroom is an important social setting and has an impact on those who spend time in it cannot be denied. Students are undoubtedly influenced by the events that take place in classrooms and are, in various degrees, influenced by the substance of the educational program; that is, the content, skills, and other learning that is presented or treated in some other way have an impact on classroom participants. Another less direct, but more pervasive and quite possibly more powerful, influence on students in classrooms is what McLuhan (5) might term the classroom medium. It consists of the techniques and procedures—both conscious and unconscious—that are used in dealing with learning and managing the classroom. It consists of classroom life itself rather than subject matter products of that life.

A major aspect of the classroom medium is social interaction—the verbal and nonverbal interchanges that take place among the classroom members. This interaction occurs between one student and another and also between the student and the teacher. Both types of interaction can have a significant effect on students. Interaction between the student and the teacher and more specifically the messages that teachers send to students are of special importance because of the nature of the teacher's position in the classroom. The teacher and the student are not equal participants in the classroom. Because of the teacher's authority, responsibility, and experience he has more power than students have. Although many teachers may try to ameliorate their power, the teacher-student relationship in classrooms is almost always a superior-subordinate relationship.

The notion the writer wishes to explore here is the possible effects of the teacher's interaction with students' achievements in reading. The complexity of the classroom prevents a comprehensive treatment of all the possible interaction factors, but two important sets of factors are herein examined: the general climate and the instructional patterns.

Classroom climate refers to the social and the emotional environment that the teacher establishes through his verbal and nonverbal contacts with students. It refers to the interpersonal relationships, the feeling tone, and the atmosphere of the classroom. Four climatic factors that can have an influence on reading achievement are teacher-student roles, expectations, teacher model, and group living.

Teacher-Student Roles

In all classrooms teachers develop certain leadership influence roles for themselves. At one end of a continuum teachers can assume an authoritarian role in which they control all activities and events that take place in the classroom. Teachers would make all of the important decisions, initiate all activities, and monopolize communication. Most of their talk would consist of telling. In short, at this end of the continuum the teacher is a dictator. At the other end of the continuum the teacher exercises no authority in the classroom at all. He makes no decisions; he does not control; he does not influence. Students are completely free to do what they wish. Any activities, talk, or experiences that take place are at the direction and control of students themselves. At this end of the continuum the teacher has chosen to be powerless.

From these two teacher roles, there is a differential effect on students. The authoritarian role causes dependence in students. They learn to do only those things they are told to do and no more. They learn to react rather than act, to parrot the thinking of others rather than to think, and to conform rather than to be curious. The authoritarian teacher by his actions tells students that they are not to be trusted, that they cannot make decisions for themselves, that their thoughts are not important, that their interests are insignificant, and, in general, that they are imperfect persons. Debilitating effects also result from the totally nonauthoritarian teacher. The teacher who relinquishes all responsibility for student growth and casts students adrift to do whatever they would like or to do nothing at all causes anxiety. To offer no direction or aid results in an inadequate self-image for students, as does to offer too much direction or aid.

The effect of the teacher role on student achievement would appear to be that authoritarian teachers tend to get lower student achievement. Although the effect of role on achievement continues to be investigated, present research evidence supports this contention. Perhaps the best known study in this regard is the one by Flanders (*1*). He found that at the junior high school level, students had lower achievement scores in mathematics and social studies when their teachers were direct in their influence rather than indirect. Direct influence consists of lecturing, giving directions, and justifying authority. It is clearly an authoritarian role. Indirect influence consists of asking questions, accepting students' ideas and feelings, and praising students. It is not the equivalent of the nonauthoritarian role sketched earlier, however. It is on the same side of the continuum as the nonauthoritarian role, but it is not that extreme. In indirect influence, teachers and students share responsibility and power.

The authoritarian teacher role, then, results in less intellectual growth as well as less social and emotional growth of students. Nevertheless, in elementary and secondary classrooms alike, the majority of teachers assume roles that are in the direction of authoritarianism. Casual observations in both classrooms and systematic studies of classroom life reveal that teachers monopolize classroom talk and that a major portion of these verbalizations is in lecturing and giving directions. Observations reveal that decision making and initiating activities are almost an exclusive prerogative of the teacher.

It seems reasonable to believe that the teacher who is closer to the nonauthoritarian side of the continuum will have students who exercise self-control, display self-confidence, and have self-esteem and that these qualities will result in venturesomeness and other qualities that will improve achievement in all areas including reading. But, how can one become less authoritarian? A good place to start is with the teacher's verbal interaction. Decreasing use of lecturing and directing and increasing use of questions, praising, and accepting would make a substantial contribution to this role change.

Expectations

Another aspect of classroom climate that can influence reading achievement are the expectations teachers have for students. Such expectations can influence achievement because of the concept of the self-fulfilling prophecy.

The self-fulfilling prophecy exists in many contexts. One can fine numerous examples of it in everyday life, in medicine, in industry, and in other areas. Simply stated, the self-fulfilling prophecy means that what one expects to happen or to be the case in interpersonal matters will indeed happen or result not only because one might have foreknowledge of the persons involved but because one's expectations influence his treatment of the persons involved and cause them to behave in the way predicted. For example, if someone meets a person for the first time and expects that he will be an open, kind person, one will treat him in that manner, and that person will, in turn, sense this openness and kindness and respond in the same way.

The importance of this phenomenon in education is illustrated by Rosenthal and Jacobson (6). These researchers set out to test whether the students for whom the teacher expected greater intellectual growth would show greater growth. By testing elementary school students with a nonverbal intelligence test disguised as a test to predict academic "blooming" and then randomly selecting 20 percent of the students and informing the teachers of the various classes that test scores indicated that these students would show unusual intellectual gains during the year, the researchers were able to support their hypothesis. When the nonverbal intelligence test was administered eight months later and test score gains were examined, it was found that the students whose teachers were told there would be noticeable gains did, indeed, show more than the other students. The gains were the highest for first and second grade students. Also, the students who were predicted to "bloom" showed greater improvement in reading than did the other students.

All teachers have expectations for students' academic progress. For some students great growth is expected; for others, average growth; and for still others, no growth at all. These expectations for success or failure are undoubtedly communicated to students in countless ways; and, consequently, the students achieve the goals that the teachers have set for them. Rosenthal and Jacobson (6) do not thoroughly describe the teacher behavior that indicated expected success or failure to students, but examples of how this behavior might occur in classroom interaction are readily available. Expected failure might be communicated by less encouragement and praise, by less attention and listening, and by less soliciting and more telling. Just the simple command "Here's a paragraph you can read, Greg" carries a great deal of meaning in terms of expected success or failure. Under the guise of meeting individual differences we often expect too little. Besides verbal communication, there is nonverbal communication and also the classroom organization in which the communication takes place. Any form of ability grouping immediately singles out some students as predicted high achievers and others as predicted low achievers. The teacher's expectations alone will have an impact on student achievement; but when one considers the fact that students sense the teacher's expectation of other students and they begin to view and treat their classmates in certain ways, the force of self-fulfilling prophecy can be seen.

To increase reading achievement for all students the self-fulfilling prophecy must be put to work in a positive way. In other words, what teachers need to do is create a success climate for students who need to believe that learning to read is really quite a simple process which all children can do. Teachers need to employ communication techniques and other procedures that tell each student that he will succeed.

Teacher Model

The model that the teacher provides for students to emulate is the third area of classroom climate that can affect learning how to read. It seems reasonable to believe that if teachers presented a literate model to which students could aspire, reading achievement would be facilitated. All too often, however, the teacher model that is presented is a nonliterate one. By their own attitudes and behaviors some teachers communicate to students that reading is an unimportant activity—e.g., by not using the printed word themselves to obtain information or pleasure. All teachers do not show that they are voluminous readers and that there are innumerable benefits for those who are. Rather than actually reading novels, magazines, and other materials in the classroom or calling attention to things they currently are reading or recently have read, teachers confine their classroom reading to classroom material. What they show students by their actions is that reading is a school tool rather than a personal tool and that, while it is necessary to be able to read to succeed in school, reading has little value beyond the school.

Closely related to literacy is intellectuality. Frequently the teacher model that is seen by students is that of a technologist rather than an intellectual. The students see an adult who is concerned with reading achievement as an end in itself. They see an adult who is interested in having students correctly associate sounds with symbols but who has minimal concern for the uses of this skill. Essentially what students learn about reading through the teacher model is how to teach it to someone else because that is what they see their teacher do. They do not learn the real uses of reading by emulating their teacher because he does not display these characteristics in the classroom. He does not satisfy his curiosity through reading, clarify his thinking through reading, collect information through reading, or formulate values through reading. In short, we expect students to become literate and scholarly, but we do not provide a literate, intellectual model for them to follow. Certainly those who work with children should strive to show through example the major purpose of reading and other school learning.

Group Living

Classroom life is group life, and the teacher reacts to this group life in certain ways. This is another area of classroom climate that can have an impact on reading achievement. According to Jackson (*4*), because teachers have to interact with twenty-five to thirty-five students in the classroom rather than with one student, delay, denial, interruption, and distraction result. Delay results because the teacher directs students to take turns. He cannot permit all students to talk at the same time during a discussion, use the same microscope, or get a drink of water in unison. Instead, explicit or implicit lines are formed, and children wait. Some lines move more slowly than others, and some never move at all. This condition causes denial. Frequently students' questions are never answered, their raised hands are ignored, and their time to work in the library is postponed. Some of the kinds of interruptions that occur because of group living are those caused by disciplining, dealing with immediate instructional problems, and adhering to time schedules. When one child is reprimanded or told where to find some particular information or resource, other students with whom the teacher may be interacting suffer interruption. When the teacher moves the class along from reading to mathematics or from science to social studies because it is ten o'clock, the whole class is probably interrupted. Distraction occurs for these same reasons, but also students are distracted simply because they have no privacy. Rarely can they get away from their classmates and the teacher.

This living-in-a-crowd results in boredom and the wasting of valuable time. Time spent in teaching and learning reading is not so productive as it could be. If undesirable effects of group living could be eliminated or reduced, it seems reasonable to believe that time would be spent more wisely and that achievement would be increased. The question is "Can something be done to deter the effects of group living? or Does group life force teachers to behave in certain ways?"

Although perhaps in some respects the teacher is powerless, there seem to be certain things the teacher can do to combat the effects of group life and create a more productive classroom climate. Teachers could, for example, give up their role as gatekeeper. Many classroom lines could be reduced by permitting students to manage themselves in the classroom. The invisible "talk line" that develops during discussion when teachers employ a democratic process for deciding who can speak and who cannot—those who have just spoken go to the back of the imaginary line—can be easily eliminated. Since all children are neither able nor really interested in making the same quality or quantity of contributions in all discussions, the teacher might interact with only a few of the students in the total group. Also, by making discussions less like recitation sessions and by encouraging student-initiated statements, as well as answers to questions, the lines could be reduced. Usually everybody is required to recite, but only interested persons discuss. Making the discussion group smaller than the total class would further reduce the "talk line." Some other ways to reduce group-living effects in classrooms are to have flexible rather than rigid time schedules and to tolerate a certain amount of disorder. Many teachers have given up on trying to know and control everything occurring in the classroom. This way they interrupt less and quite possibly their students achieve more.

INSTRUCTIONAL PATTERNS

The second group of interaction forces that could have an impact on achievement in reading is the instructional factors or the actual teaching procedures that teachers use or could use in teaching reading. In the present context, instructional factors refer to the verbal and nonverbal interchanges that take place among the teacher and students during the teaching of reading. Two of these factors are techniques and cognitive level.

Techniques

A great variety of ways or methods of teaching reading exists, and each of these methods contains its own set of operating procedures. The basal reading approach, which appears to be the most widely used method, consists of a variety of activities: vocabulary review, introduction of new terms, skill building exercises, introduction of the new story, and comprehension activities. Teachers may not follow this exact sequence, but their deviations from it are slight. How the teacher carries out these activities constitutes the instructional techniques.

The Impact of Classroom Interaction

The trouble with the activities of the basal method or of any other method of teaching reading along with the instructional techniques used to implement the method is that they often become routinized and stereotyped. And the routine leads to boredom and disinterest.

To have to progress day after day through the vocabulary review to the new vocabulary to all the other activities must have an impact on students' interest in learning to read. The manner in which the teacher interacts with students during these sessions may have even greater impact. During the introduction of new vocabulary, teachers invariably do the same things. They ask questions such as: "How many syllables are there, Bob?" "What's the short 'a' sound, Sandy?" "Who wants to try this one?" "Can you think of a synonym for that term?" These questions in themselves are not inappropriate; but when they are inevitable, they can have an unfavorable influence on students.

In addition to the formal vocabulary activity, these same questions are asked of students when during oral or silent reading of a story they indicate that they do not know a certain word. Here the questions have another effect. They are an additional source of interruption and delay. The teacher's primary concern is for the student to be able to say the word on his own. The student's involvement in the story is of less importance.

Techniques in basal reading instruction are not the only ones that are routinized and can cause boredom. Many of the same techniques are used in nearly all the approaches to teaching reading. Other techniques that are peculiar to a given reading method often make up a new set of routines.

To make reading instruction alive and exciting, teachers must strive to make their techniques alive and exciting. Certainly one of the ways to do this is to broaden one's technique repertory and to use a variety of techniques as many successful teachers of reading have done. Using the example of vocabulary again, at times a teacher may want to use questions in an attempt to have the student discover the word himself; but at other times the teacher may just tell him the word, have students work in pairs, or forget about the new terms altogether. Another suggestion to reduce the impact of the reading routine is to reduce the time spent on reading instruction. One of the reasons that the techniques appear so rigid is that students are exposed to them at length. Reading teaching techniques are used not only for an hour or two every day in the formal reading period but often continuously throughout the day in all subject areas. It is not unusual to make social studies, science, and other subject areas quasireading instruction periods.

Cognitive Level

Along with instructional techniques, the factor of cognitive level can be a strong influence on students' becoming able readers and achievers in other areas as well. There are many schemes to conceptualize cognition in the classroom. Most of these focus on thought levels ranging from recall of facts to evaluative thinking. An example of one of these schemes is that developed by Gallagher (2). It consists of four cognitive levels and one noncognitive category: cognitive-memory thinking (recall of facts and other information); convergent thinking (solving problems); divergent thinking (creating or generating ideas in data-poor situations); evaluative thinking (judging or rating ideas and events); and routine (noncognitive acts such as calling on students, making assignments, and praising work). When teacher-verbal behavior in the classroom is classified with such a scheme in some systematic way, the results are that the predominant cognitive level at which the classroom operates is memory or recall. Numerous studies attest to this finding [see Guzak on reading instruction (3)]. The levels that receive limited use, in Gallagher's terms, are divergent and evaluative thinking. These cognitive levels are often totally absent in the classroom.

Reading teachers need to examine their cognitive levels of operation because there is a close relationship between the level of their verbalizations and the level of students' verbalizations. This condition is particularly true concerning questions. If teachers ask memory questions, students will give memory answers. If teachers ask for evaluation, students will give evaluative replies.

There is no question that facts are important in reading and that if one cannot recall the facts that he has read, he is not a proficient reader. To spend a majority of the time on factual recall, when dealing with comprehension in reading groups, or to make the most of the written questions or comprehension exercises dealing with factual recall, that a teacher may require a student to do, is unwise because the recall of facts is a superficial level of understanding. Students would gain much greater meaning from what they read if they dealt with the materials on a convergent, divergent, and evaluative basis. If through teacher questions and teacher statements implications, predictions, applications, values, feelings, and other areas were explored, students' understanding would be increased immeasurably. Further, if the teacher were functioning at the higher cognitive levels, direct solicitation of facts would be unnecessary. Recall of facts is essential for evaluating, creating, and the other higher cognitive levels. If a student can think at these higher levels, the teacher can be assured that the student's recall skills are adequate.

Another advantage of stressing the higher cognitive levels is that, as in the case of teacher modeling, the student is exposed to the real purpose of reading. He comes to see reading as something more than preparation for either oral or written classroom catechism. If we wish students to become able readers, we need to stress the higher cognitive levels in addition to employing vibrant and changing instructional techniques.

Social interaction as well as the total classroom medium is a force that needs to be understood and employed for student benefit. Climate factors, instructional factors, and other factors can influence student achievement in reading and the other subject areas. Although many successful teachers intuitively provide a healthy, trusting climate for students and utilize exciting instructional procedures, perhaps all teachers could benefit from an examination of their classroom interaction. They will then come to know both the facilitating and destructive aspects of their communication and quite possibly begin to consciously use those behaviors that will contribute to an effective classroom medium and to discard all of the other behaviors.

References

1. Flanders, Ned A. *Teacher Influence, Pupil Attitudes, and Achievement.* U. S. Office of Education, Cooperative Research Project, No. 397. Minneapolis: University of Minnesota, 1960.
2. Gallagher, James J. *Productive Thinking of Gifted Children.* U. S. Office of Education, Cooperative Research Project, No. 965. Urbana: University of Illinois, 1965.
3. Guzak, Frank J. "Teacher Questioning and Reading," *Elementary English,* 42 (1965), 559-568.
4. Jackson, Philip W. *Life in Classrooms.* New York: Holt, Rinehart and Winston, 1968.
5. McLuhan, Marshall, and Quentin Fiore. *The Medium Is the Massage.* New York: Bantam Books, 1967.
6. Rosenthal, Robert, and Lenore Jacobson. *Pygmalion in the Classroom: Teacher Expectation and Pupils' Intellectual Development.* New York: Holt, Rinehart and Winston, 1968.

Reading and Values

Alex Molnar

There are any number of reading programs and variations available to school systems, and each has its advocates and detractors. With disagreements among experts so sharp and much of the professional language so imposing, it is risky business for a nonexpert to raise questions for reading specialists to consider. However, to do so is precisely the writer's purpose because, in his opinion, the issues involved, while of deep concern to reading specialists, do transcend their field of expertise.

It is often all too easy to be drawn into a debate over the relative merits of one method of teaching reading over another and to lose sight of why people should read in the first place, as well as to lose sight of the purpose of teaching reading in our schools: The acquisition of language largely defines what it means to be human. Language is man's primary tool for investing his life with meaning; without language he could not have created the knowledge and the technology that he has. Reading, however, is only one part of the larger process of developing the capacity for a symbolic representation of reality.

Virtually all students who enter school already possess an amazing range of motor and conceptual skills and abilities which enable them to communicate orally. Yet, they have not been taught to talk in any formal sense. There is no national educational commitment to the "right to speak." There is no crisis for educators to address themselves to. If it is a fact that most students enter our schools talking, it is also a fact that comparatively few enter knowing how to read—a condition which elementary schools devote most of their energies to changing. In our society, learning to talk is a process recognized as being subject to individual control while learning to read is an institutional problem, toward which solution millions of dollars have been allocated.

62

The shift in focus from the individual to the institution provides the basis for the imposition of systematic external controls on the act of learning to read. Transferring language development from an individual responsibility to an institutional commitment generates a series of value potentials operating within a dynamic of social, educational, institutional, and personal interaction.

A distinction between individuals learning to read and programs designed to teach reading within the institutional contest of our schools must be maintained. All schools, regardless of their organization, represent contrived environments which reflect certain value priorities, as well as implicit or explicit assumptions about how teaching and learning are most effectively facilitated. It is deceptively easy to say that schools are for educating people and not to touch on the question of the end toward which people are being educated.

What goes on in schools can be seen in at least three ways, each of which has a different set of implications for reading programs, embodies different assumptions, and involves different value combinations. These ways of conceptualizing the various functions of formal education are best stated in simple propositional form: 1) schools are for training, 2) schools are for schooling, and 3) schools are for education.

These propositions are undoubtedly true of all schools to some extent; however, all three cannot be given equal priority in any school. Recognizing that not one of these propositions completely describes any school, abstracting them for study should nonetheless sharpen the distinctions in the value orientations of each. First, however, must come definitions of training, schooling, and education as they are used here:

Training is a process through which individuals acquire a well-defined set of externally verifiable skills. Competence is certified by an external agent upon the demonstration of these skills in prescribed manner.

Schooling is a process of establishing and regulating patterns of student behavior for the purposes of maintaining the institutional organization of the school. Adequacy is assessed on the basis of an individual's ability to conform to prescribed behavior patterns.

Education is the process of creating meaning through individual learning. The adequacy of education is self-verified by the individual.

SCHOOLS ARE FOR TRAINING

If we assume schools are for training, then we can regard teaching reading primarily from the point of view of skill acquisition. Reading is seen as a series of skills to be mastered and to be best taught in a highly organized and prescribed manner. Just as airline pilots or surgeons are trained to acquire skills which they will later use in their vocations, so children are taught skills which they will use sometime in the future. The orientation is essentially "then" and "there" rather than "here" and "now," and the skills and knowledge to be acquired are seen as existing separate from the student. Materials are developed primarily for their facility in providing an opportunity to acquire and practice certain well-defined skills; the materials need not in themselves be of any other particular value.

In many primary readers the stories tell no story. Remove the pictures and we are left with a word list in sentence form. The content is unappealing in itself; it does, however, provide opportunities for word recognition and other skill development. For example, consider the following story, "Suzy Wants to Work," from a basal reader (6) in use in some Milwaukee public schools:

> "I want to work," said Suzy.
> "I can get up and help you work.
> See me get up and help."
> "Get down, Suzy," said Larry.
> "Get down and come here.
> Father and I can work.
> You can look."
> "Come here, Suzy," said Father.
> "You can help me.
> Here is something for you."
> "Here I go, Father," said Larry.
> "I want Mother to come and see.
> I can run and get Mother."
> "Come in, Mother," said Larry.
> "Come in and see something."
> "Mother, Mother," said Suzy.
> "Larry and Father can work.
> And I can help.
> Come and see something funny.
> See something for Larry and me."

Such a story seems incapable of generating any real student interest which creates meaning. Often the comment that children *cannot* read is a cover up for the real problem that many children *will not* read materials in which they are not interested and cannot become involved.

Training by its nature requires practice and demands discipline imposed either from within or without. Very few primary age children exhibit a willingness to discipline themselves in the practice of reading skills; therefore, programs in this model are rigidly structured with specific tasks imposed on the children by the material. While the teacher retains responsibility for the overall direction of the classroom, some materials in this model purport to be teacher proof. The Bereiter-Englemann program, for example, provides for ". . . brief but intensive periods of drill in language, reading, and arithmetic skills, using almost militaristic procedures which demand a high and continuous level of participation from all children" (2). Such programs fit nicely, though not necessarily, into a compensatory model of education. The rationale frequently articulated for the use of these programs with disadvantaged children is that in a formal sense it is necessary to provide those skills which these children's advantaged counterparts have already acquired informally by virtue of their family background and social environment. One source of the major critiques of compensatory education has been the supporters of a training model. They argue that the attempt on the part of some programs to focus on environmental enrichment in general rather than concentrating on delivering the skills students need to improve academic achievement does not enhance appreciably a student's chances or success in school. The question of success in school leads to the second proposition.

SCHOOLS ARE FOR SCHOOLING

If we assume schools are for schooling, then we must examine reading programs in terms of their relationship to the institutional setting within which they operate. Nadel (*20*) points out that educational institutions are largely regulative; i.e., institutions which bear

> ... upon the operation of other institutions . . . (they achieve their) purpose or task in enabling the purpose and task of other institutions to be achieved; so that *the regulative institution does not merely represent the "moulds and channels," of behavior* (for this is characteristic of all institutions), *but safeguards them.* [Emphasis mine.]

Reading programs viewed from this perspective are to be valued for two virtues: the extent to which they impart to students' skills necessary for satisfactory academic achievement and the degree to which their patterns or organization reinforce and support the institutional norms of the school. Reading programs must possess both these virtues to be valued in this context. In his column Kirk (*13*) illustrates this point. He quotes a teacher who has found a phonics system of teaching reading to be effective but her success, a source of frustration.

> I am able to have half of my first graders advanced enough by February or March to slide easily and eagerly into second grade work—with no bother to anyone, as I take them myself as far as they can go by the end of May.

> The hangup, of course, is that the teacher who will have them next cannot (will not and is not permitted to) start them where they left off . . . . The establishment in Texas is dead set against it. And we in the Catholic schools must do just what the public schools do and let these bright kids drag their weary way through eight grades.

If we accept for a moment the contention that this teacher has found a method of teaching reading that is quite effective for her, it becomes quite clear that whatever the merits of her program in the abstract—i.e., students effectively learning to read—it is deficient because its implementation threatens institutional norms, which have nothing to do with children learning to read. These norms exist because they serve to maintain the school's pattern of organization and in so doing assure not only the efficient functioning of the school but also that students, upon leaving the school system, will be socialized to the point of being easily assimilated into other social institutions. All this matter need not seem sinister since without people able to function in the context of social institutions there can be no social organization. It does indicate, however, that reading programs are subject to judgment on the basis of criteria (implicit or explicit) which have little or nothing to do with the act of learning to read.

If schools are for schooling, then academic achievement becomes a tool for enforcing the values of the system and not a reflection of individual learning. Anyone who has spent time in schools knows that reading achievement scores are a primary method of grouping students, describing them, and relating to them from the earliest grades. Materials are valued for their ability to facilitate the classification of students and not for content per se. In this respect, training and schooling models overlap. If schools are for schooling, training is highly valued because it provides a clear specification of what skills are to be acquired and equally clear, observable evidence that they have or have not been acquired. Such clarity and organization are necessary for classification. If schools are for schooling, then the primary role of the individual is to fit in and adopt a then-and-there orientation toward the usefulness of the experience which he is having.

SCHOOLS ARE FOR EDUCATION

If we assume schools are for education, then reading programs must be examined primarily for the extent to which they promote individual learning. In viewing reading programs this way, the distinction between teaching, achievement, and learning assumes great importance. It is possible to define teaching and achievement quite specifically and in operational terms. Learning, on the other hand, may be a result of teaching and may be reflected in school achievement, but not necessarily. Learning, a function of the interaction between an individual and his environment, is an intensely personal act. Since learning is under individual control, then knowledge, insight, understanding, and meaning exist as curricular potentials, which require individual self-validation to call them forth in concrete and particular form. It is here that the conception that school is for education breaks sharply with the conceptions that school is for training or that school is for schooling. These conceptions require a value priority on individual and collective actions which can be and are subject to external control. Knowledge, insight, understanding, and meaning are implied to exist only to the degree to which they can be externally verified, i.e., by teacher observation or test performance.

The content of reading materials is extremely important if we hold that schools are for education. They are valued not only for the skills they help develop but for the meanings they suggest and opportunities for self-verification they provide. The orientation of a reading program in this model is primarily here and now rather than then and there; that is, reading and learning to read are seen as pleasurable and personally useful acts as they are done. Learning to read is not something one must endure with the promise of future pleasure or benefit.

Determining which conception of the nature of schools shall be addressed by reading programs represents one level of value priority. There are, however, others to be considered. It is suggested earlier in this paper that there is no national commitment to a "Right to Speak." Let's use that example again to illustrate a point. To hold that people have a right to speak is also to believe they have a right to be heard. Both speaking and listening derive meaning only in their interaction. The act of talking makes little sense divorced from the act of listening. Transferring this logic to the Right to Read, it would appear that if people have a right to read, then they also have a right to read or not to read that which is meaningful to them. From these assumptions two fundamental value issues arise concerning the nature of the content of reading materials and the classroom organization that reading programs call for.

The content of reading materials, whether used primarily for their usefulness as a vehicle for skill development or for their substance, communicates values to the reader. It cannot be assumed that instructional materials do not have an effect upon the attitudes children hold. Even materials not explicitly developed to effect attitudes can and do. One of the characteristics of human beings as opposed to other animals is the extent to which their learning is polyphasic. Humans tend to learn more than one thing at a time. Selection of materials for a given purpose does not deny the potential for significant other learning from them—intended or not.

A focus on values in the study of educational processes has implications not only for understanding the organization of behavior but also for understanding polyphasic learning, since education, the fundamental organizing process, occurs always in the context of values, and teachers are usually teaching values by implication, regardless of the immediate subject matter (7).

Thus, regardless of the explicit purpose of instructional materials in reading programs (skill development, for example) we must be conscious of the value implications of both the content and the organization it requires. Two content themes—sexism and racism—illustrate this point.

Sexism

The story quoted earlier, "Suzy Wants to Work," makes little sense as a story without its accompanying pictures. Despite the lack of a coherent story line, the message conveyed is implicit by sexism:

> "Come in, Mary," said Larry.
> "Come in and see something."
> "Mother, Mother," said Suzy.
> "Larry and Father can work and I can help."

While the stated purpose of reading programs is not the development of sex stereotypes in children, a study of children's readers in use in New Jersey reveals some interesting statistics:

There were 88 biographies of men and 17 biographies of women.

There were 146 occupations portrayed by adult males and 25 occupations portrayed by adult females (including a circus fat lady).

An analysis of themes in the same study reveals that boys characteristically are portrayed as possessing desirable traits while girls are not.

To wit:

Active Mastery Themes	Boys	Girls
1. Ingenuity, cleverness	131	33
2. Industry, problem solving ability	169	47
3. Strength, bravery, heroism	143	36
4. Routine helpfulness	53	68
Elective or creative helpfulness	54	19
5. Apprenticeship, acquisition of skills, coming of age	151	53
6. Earning, acquisition, unearned rewards	87	19
7. Adventure, exploration, and imaginative play	216	68

Second Sex Themes	Boys	Girls
1. Passivity and pseudodependence	19	119
2. Altruism	55	22
3. Goal constriction and rehearsal for domesticity	50	166
4. Incompetence, mishaps	51	60
5. Victimization and humiliation of the opposite sex	7	68

Girls and women are systematically excluded from almost all but stereotyped roles in children's readers, and the language of the readers strongly supports these stereotypes. Consider the following quotes.

1. "Look at her, Mother, just look at her. She is just like a girl. She gives up" (21).

2. "Mrs. Allen shuddered. To think that her boy had killed such a creature made her a bit proud, but also just a little bit faint" (16).

3. "Kites are for boys; kites are not for girls" (17).

4. "Oh, Raymond, boys are much braver than girls" (1).

The materials cited are intended to teach reading; there can, however, be little doubt that they convey more than reading skills (24).

It can be argued that research does, in fact, indicate different aptitudes among male and female students; however, one researcher after reviewing the literature commented that ". . . by the time such differences do clearly emerge, the child has received a considerable amount of sex role training" (2).

Sex stereotyping is not a concern of women alone. The value implicit in such stereotyped portrayals has an impact on boys and men as well. Jourard (11), for example, links the male role with the higher and earlier mortality rate of men. The feminists in children's literature legitimately ask that "words like 'sissy'— and 'hero' too—should be dissected and exposed for the inhuman demands they make on growing boys." And they offer suggestions for reviewing the content of books for sexist messages:

> In our view, a non-sexist portrayal would offer the girl reader a positive image of woman's physical, emotional, and intellectual potential—one that would encourage her to reach her own full personhood, free of tradition- ally imposed limitations (5).

While it may be true that sex stereotyping in instructional materials is simply a reflection of sex stereotyping in society at large, the implication of the school in the formation, transmission, and reinforcement of such stereotyping cannot be denied. Educators who specialize in reading should perhaps consider the possibility that the very materials they use to help children gain control over their lives and extend their freedom are subtly telling children that their poten- tial is severely limited and that the nature of their contributions to society is sharply prescribed at birth.

Racism

Unlike sexism which has entered our consciousness comparatively recently (at least the consciousness of most males), racism has been an out-front issue for over a decade. Accepting for a moment that some progress has been made in terms of integrating instructional materials, it is still necessary to examine this progress not only quantitatively but qualitatively, as well as in terms of its direction. An analysis of the political decision concerning the development of materials, with large scale adoption in mind as well as the problem of the continued use of outdated materials (in some instances more than two decades old) in some school systems, lies far beyond the scope of this paper.

The quantitative progress in including minority groups in instructional mate- rials need not give us cause for rejoicing. In 1947 the American Council on Education reported that intergroup conflict was more of a threat to our society than some foreign source and called upon educators to face their responsibility in meeting this challenge. Yet, in a study of the treatment of minorities in social studies texts in 1969, Kane (12) found that none of the texts he surveyed met criteria which would

1. Present a pluralistic—rather than a 100 percent white, Protestant, Anglo-Saxon—view of history and the current scene.

2. Portray minority groups not as "out groups"—strange, different, and isolated—but sympathetically and in depth as valuable, dynamic, contributing elements in our culture.

3. Deal frankly with past and current barriers to full equality in citizenship and constructive intergroup relations and with ongoing attempts to achieve both civil and human rights for all.

And he concludes in part that

The message is apparent; we can no longer appeal to the reason and conscience of those who supply our textbooks. Action must be taken by the concerned consumers of those goods (i.e., the teacher, the parent, and the student). If schools and parents continue to be satisfied with the best available texts rather than demanding those that *fully* meet the criteria their use demands, improvements will not be forthcoming. The continued use of mediocre texts will guarantee the persistence of mediocrity.

The study cited is not of materials used in reading programs. It is reasonable, however, to assume that if publishers have not met the three criteria of adequacy for social studies texts—texts whose substance should be designed to explicitly deal with such social issues as race relations—, they are also likely to be found lacking in their treatment of race in reading materials whose content is not so dramatically to the point. This factor seems to be borne out even by a casual examination of some of the reading materials in use in Milwaukee.

How shall we define progress? Does the inclusion of black, tan, yellow, or red skins in children's reading materials represent progress? Perhaps not. Indeed the inclusion of various ethnic groups within the context of a white middle-class setting may be harmful for two reasons. Meil and Kiester (*18*) report that

Passion for conformity seems to be a . . . trait which affects the suburban child's feelings toward "different" people. Our studies show clearly that he takes a dim view of anyone—adults, children, even himself—who deviates from the norm, and that he places a premium on being exactly what adults want him to be.

Stories such as "Suzy Wants to Work" probably tend to support conformist values in white middle-class children while at the same time they communicate negative messages of difference—inferiority in children who do not share the norms.

. . . most ghetto schools confront black children with a curriculum and a set of learning conditions which do not relate to the students' life outside of school. Textbooks and procedures are developed by and for whites and have little relevance to black parents with a Southern rural background, or their ghetto raised children.

From the classroom to the PTA [black children] discover that the school does not like them, does not respond to them, does not appreciate their culture, and does not think they can learn (*14*).

Olsen (*22*) touches on a key question for reading teachers and other educators in determining the direction to move in developing multiracial materials.

A deep conviction of education generally has been the belief that ethnic differences should always be ignored, or at least minimized, while all possible similarities are constantly emphasized. Children of all backgrounds are still *children*, it is forcefully argued, and their ethnic differences, after all, are really superficial. Of course, the cultural contributions of various groups should be praised on appropriate occasions such as Brotherhood Week, and special provisions must surely be made for Spanish-speaking and culturally disadvantaged children. But at all times concepts and feelings of commonality and of psychological identification with the whole human race should be stressed. This view holds that ethnic differences must be "understood," "accepted," even "tolerated" (as somewhat unfortunate deviations from the dominant and desirable norm), but that such differences should not be highlighted in school—of all places!

The question raised by Olsen's statement has largely been ignored. Typically, instructional materials deal with ethnic differences by transplanting minority group members into a white setting.

An example of portraying minority groups in white middle-class settings can be found in *Lippincott's Basic Reader* for grades one and two. In these readers the publishers have inserted two stories: one at each grade level which portrays blacks in a middle-class setting in a story in which black faces make no difference. These books were copyrighted in 1964 and 1969 and will probably be in use into the 1980s. Realistically, social and educational transformation cannot be an overnight process, but equally realistically educators must continue to ask themselves whether they are, in fact, willing to demand instructional materials which do not explicitly or by omission deal adequately with ethnic differences. Perhaps we should even begin to ask ourselves whether the ethnic background of textbook authors is a source of concern, along with the racial composition of the publishing houses.

Are minority authors writing stories for childrens' readers? Are minority members represented in decision making positions in publishing houses? are there textbooks available from minority publishing houses and minority authors which can effectively be used in school reading programs? Perhaps it is true that a good story is a good story, whether written by a white or a minority group member. Perhaps it is true that children of all races can enjoy such good stories. Perhaps it is true that the racial makeup of the board of directors of a publishing house is of no concern to educators. But only perhaps. Do we as educators wish to commit ourselves to a vision of a society in which there is only one correct norm for people of differing backgrounds? If not, we must ask ourselves whether white control over the materials children read from authorship to adoption is a condition which has the potential for generating a vision of a pluralistic multiracial society in the children we seek to educate. Are we content to let commentaries such as the following describe the reading material we use as effectively as it describes the TV show it was written to review?

So far, the plot hasn't really gone out into the streets, where there is material rich enough to float a thousand sit-coms, and of course ten times as many tragedies. It hasn't exploited its chosen milieu—not just the store front church, the welfare system, the numbers game, the militant sect; but the energy, music and art as well—and, like *Julia*, it seems locked into a benign Moynihanism. (Widow and widower are substituted for the absent wife or husband.) Why not try young black writers like Ishmael Reed and Cecil Brown? Or, if you have to have an older one, Chester Himes? They could provide the wild humor and dark meanings missing from *Sanford and Son . . . (3)*.

Perhaps educators ought to question whether "melting pot" is an adequate description of or goal for our society. Perhaps another metaphor such as "symphony orchestra," as Olsen has recommended, would be more suggestive.

ORGANIZATION COMMUNICATES VALUE MESSAGES

If the Right to Read also means the right to read that which is meaningful, then from a larger social point of view educators have failed. They have failed because of the few materials to which students have access that can be judged worthy on any basis other than as platforms for teaching skills.

Often negative value messages are communicated implicitly by existing reading materials, supported by the absence of materials which communicate other values. The developer of reading materials, reading teachers, and educators in general cannot ignore the value implications of the curriculum they develop and use.

The value shaping process is of particular interest to those in schools who are responsible for curriculum process and materials. . . . Curriculum materials such as course outlines, books, audiovisual aids, etc., determine to a large degree the access learners have to the content areas of human enlightenment. Curriculum process and materials, then, shape values by producing them, by setting the stage for learning events, and by providing the ground rules for action in the learning area. Both the quality and the quantity of value sharing experiences are determined to a large degree by the planned provision of a curriculum context for learners which shapes— but which also may selectively deny—values (23).

Illich (9) pointedly asks:

. . . shall we set up only those institutional arrangements that protect the autonomy of the learner—his private initiative to decide what he will learn and his inalienable right to learn what he likes rather than what is useful to somebody else.

Reading and Values

Reading programs have characteristically answered "no." They have developed around a rationale which holds that reading is a tool—an indispensible tool—and while children often do not like the control to which they must submit to acquire reading skills, such control is justified because once the skills have been acquired, the child is then "free" and may read and enjoy the skills he possesses.

This rationale fits nicely into a training or schooling vision of schools and the values inherent in such a vision. However, for several reasons it is in conflict with a belief that schools are for education. Such a rationale says

1. Knowledge is an object external to the learner, not the process of assigning meaning.

2. The control of learning is external, not internal.

3. Learning is subject to regularized institutional demands, not individual spurts, leaps, and digressions.

4. The responsibility for student learning is directly that of the teacher, not the student.

5. What is learned in school is not useful here and now, but at some time in the future.

6. Individual worth is a function of knowing what is important to others rather than to one's self.

It supports these values when students are required to

1. Read materials they have not selected or to select from a prescribed list.

2. Read for the teacher and be evaluated on any of several criteria.

3. Read only when they are allowed to by the teacher.

4. Read aloud in front of others.

5. Belong to a group defined by reading test scores.

It is no longer adequate to say, "I am interested in teaching the boys and girls of America to read." Educators concerned with the teaching of reading and educators in general can no longer ignore the values they are promoting by their vision of what schools are for and the content and organization of the instructional materials they use. It is our responsibility to determine and clearly state what it is we stand for and how we shall pursue our vision.

References and Notes

1. Audio play about rainmaking. Eldonna Everetts and Byron H. Van Roekel (Eds.), *Trade Winds.* Evanston, Illinois: Harper and Row, 1966, 422.

2. Boocock, Sarane S. *An Introduction to the Sociology of Learning.* Boston: Houghton Mifflin, 1972.

3. Cyclops. "Black Sit-Com, But Too Tame," *Life,* April 21, 1972.

4. Dolmatch, Theodore B. "Color Me Brown—I'm Integrated," *Saturday Review,* September 11, 1965.

5. Feminists on Children's Literature. "A Feminist Look at Children's Books," *School Library Journal,* January 1971.

6. *Four Seasons with Suzy.* Chicago: Follett, 1965.

7. Henry, Jules. *On Education.* New York: Vintage Books, 1972.

8. Howes, Virgil. "The Trouble with Johnny," *School Library Journal,* 16 (May 1970).

9. Illich, Ivan. "After Deschooling, What?" *Social Policy,* September/October 1971.

10. *Interracial Books for Children.* Council on Interracial Books for Children, 3 (Autumn 1971).

11. Jourard, Sidney M. *The Transparent Self.* New York: Van Nostrand Reinhold, 1971.

12. Kane, Michael E. *Minorities in Textbooks: A Study of Their Treatment in Social Studies Texts.* Chicago: Quadrangle Books, 1970.

13. Kirk, Russell. "Johnny Still Can't Read," *Milwaukee Journal,* March 24, 1972.

14. Knowles, Louis L., and Kenneth Prewitt (Eds.). *Institutional Racism in America.* Englewood Cliffs, New Jersey: Prentice-Hall, 1969.

15. Larrick, Nancy. "The All-White World of Children's Books," *Saturday Review,* September 11, 1965.

16. Lippincott's Basic Reading, Teacher's Edition, H. Book, 1970, 64.

17. McKee, Paul, et al (Eds.). *Jack and Janet.* Boston: Houghton Mifflin, 1966, 132.

18. Meil, Alice, with Edwin Kiester. *The Shortchanged Children of Suburbia.* New York: Institute of Human Relations Press, 1967.

19. Missouri Commission on Human Rights. *A Survey of Textbooks Used in Missouri High Schools.* Columbia: Missouri Commission on Human Rights, 1968.

20. Nadel, S. F. *The Foundations of Social Anthropology.* Glencoe, Illinois: Free Press, 1951.

21. O'Donnel, Mabel (Ed.). *Around the Corner.* Evanston, Illinois: Harper and Row, 1966, 45, 66.

22. Olsen, Edward G. "Shall We Teach Ethnic Differences?" *Phi Delta Kappan,* 49 (May 1969).

23. Rucker, Ray W. "A Value Oriented Framework for Education and Behavioral Science," *Journal of Value Inquiry,* 3 (Winter 1969).

24. Women on Words and Images. *Dick and Jane as Victims.* Princeton, New Jersey: Women on Words and Images, 1972.

Final Comment

The statements end where they began—with a plea to recognize the social forces which impinge upon learning to read and they remind us that we are professionals concerned with the education of the young and not simply technicians concerned about training.

As professionals we are expected to bring our intelligence to bear upon the basis of reading problems and to project plans and activities to help solve our dilemmas.

Analogies can be misleading, but one is tempted to use the field of medicine as a professional analogy at this point. It would seem that social perspectives on reading can conclude (as medicine has) that an "ounce of prevention is worth a pound of cure." Like many doctors, we see the patient after he is "ill" when it may be infinitely more difficult and costly to help him than it would have been to prevent the problem in the first place.

What we need is a campaign to help prevent reading problems and to put reading in proper perspective, both in society and in the education of the individual. As concerned professionals committed to the education of the young, we might consider the following:

1. Put time, money, and effort into adult (parent) education about the environmental effects in early childhood upon later reading achievement.
2. Put time, effort, and money in positive programs and/or experiences for infants and very young children.
3. Organize, support, and lobby for social policy which eliminates poverty.
4. Organize, support, and lobby for social policies and efforts to reduce class and race differences in our society.
5. Broaden and revise school curricula to allow for multisensory learning and multimedia teaching.

6. Construct learning environments which recognize the social and environmental influences upon learning and which reflect a concept of education rather than training.

Whatever these suggestions are worth, they do get at the causes of problems and they broaden our vision beyond the absurdity of methodological solutions. They are offered here as directional possibilities in the hope that learning to read as an integral part of one's education may come to serve the best interests of each person and the goals of a truly democratic society where practical access to learning potential is not determined long before schooling.

JBM

Final Comment

DATE DUE